W9-CMJ-837

GUSTAV MAHLER

Da Capo Press Music Reprint Series

General Editor

FREDERICK FREEDMAN

Vassar College

GUSTAV MAHLER

by BRUNO WALTER

Translated by JAMES GALSTON

With a Biographical Essay by
ERNST KŘENEK

DA CAPO PRESS · NEW YORK · 1970

A Da Capo Press Reprint Edition

This Da Capo Press edition of Bruno Walter's *Gustav Mahler* is an unabridged republication of the first edition published in New York in 1941.

Library of Congress Catalog Card Number 78-87691

SBN 306-71701-8

Published by Da Capo Press
A Division of Plenum Publishing Corporation
227 West 17th Street, New York, N.Y. 10011

Manufactured in the United States of America

GUSTAV MAHLER

GUSTAV MAHLER
Etching by Arthur Paunzen

BRUNO WALTER

GUSTAV MAHLER

Translated by JAMES GALSTON

With a Biographical Essay

by

ERNST KŘENEK

THE GREYSTONE PRESS

New York

TYPOGRAPHY, PRINTING, AND BINDING IN THE U. S. A. BY
KINGSPORT PRESS, INC., KINGSPORT, TENNESSEE

CONTENTS

PAGE

Preface ix

RECOLLECTION

First Meeting 3

Hamburg 10

Steinbach 22

Vienna 33

Last Years 55

REFLECTION

Re-Creative Work 67

At the Head of the Opera . . . 67

The Conductor 78

Creative Work 88

Personality 128

GUSTAV MAHLER BY ERNST KŘENEK

Bohemian, Jew, German, Austrian . . 157

Mahler and Bruckner 161

Odyssey Through Operatic Province . . 167

PAGE
Prague and Leipzig 170
Professional Dilemma 173
Operas 176
Budapest 179
Hamburg 185
Foretokens of Surrealism 191
Mahler and Strauss 195
Mahler in Vienna 197
Life in Vienna 200
On the Threshold of "New" Music . . 205
Mahler Leaves Vienna 209
Mahler and America 211
Exit 218

INDEX 221

LIST OF ILLUSTRATIONS

Portrait Etching of Gustav Mahler by Arthur Paunzen . . . . . *Frontispiece*

Caricatures by Boehler of Gustav Mahler Conducting 84

Portrait Bust of Gustav Mahler by Auguste Rodin 156

Caricature of Gustav Mahler by Enrico Caruso 196

Preface

FOR MANY YEARS, INCLINATION AND A SENSE *of duty have urged me to speak of Gustav Mahler. Checked at every attempt by the insufficiency of the word when measured by the mystery of the existence of so great a musician, I had not got beyond a few occasional essays. And now the thirtieth recurrence of the day of his death calls upon me to say what I have to say, or else for ever hold my tongue. To be sure, after so many years of personal friendship with Mahler, and after another quarter of a century of being occupied with his work, there is much on my mind that urgently demands to be put into words. But how to satisfy the urge without running the risk of being wrecked upon the task of describing in mere words the nature of the man and of his work? My professional activity in the service of Mahler's creative work is here rather a hindrance than an advantage. For every performance shows me anew how much more directly and convincingly Mahler may be interpreted with the baton than with the word. But what if I should direct the light not upon him but upon myself? If I should simply try to tell what the work and its creator were and still are to me? Experience and thought have made a picture of Gustav Mahler develop within me which, by means of self-analysis, I hope to be able to project outwards. Well do I realize that the result of such a method can be but a highly subjective representation, which surely will be afflicted with the shortcomings of one-sidedness and incompleteness but, on the other hand, perhaps also have the advantage of reliability and the power of conviction with which one is able to speak of oneself.*

True, it is not a biography that can be produced in that manner, for I do not find within myself an account of the great transitions of his life from childhood to death, nor of the great wealth of his experiences, nor am I even able to bring home to my mind the development of the man from the age of thirty-four, when I first met him, until he had reached the fifties. Biography describes a growth; and since man "grows" by the world that surrounds him, the biographer must include in the picture of life the parental home, childhood, years of development, time, and contemporaries. I shall have to leave to a more competent man such a biographical delineation of Mahler's rich existence. As for myself, I considered the only task admitting of achievement, a description of his "being," that is to say, a reproduction of the picture of Mahler that I carry within me.

That is the reason why, in this book, only the one man appears of whom it treats, and no mention is made even of the beloved wife who so strongly influenced him, nor of the loyal sister who shared his life up to the time of his marriage, nor of the noble friends to whom he was attached to the day of his death. A description of these personal relations would be biographical, and thus contrary to the style of this book. For the same reason, I have denied myself the privilege of writing about his cultural surroundings. My exclusive theme is: What I experienced with Mahler and how I see him.

If, occasionally, I am seen to pause in my recollection to give way to reflection and then to halt in the reflection for the purpose of verifying it by some newly arising recollection, I have yet, in the main, tried to separate recollection and reflection in my endeavor to give an adequate conception of the prodigious event which Mahler's existence represents in the cultural life of our day.

RECOLLECTION

First Meeting

FROM THE DEPTHS OF MEMORY I CALL UP the picture of Gustav Mahler as he first appeared to me, then a youth of eighteen. A shout of indignation had gone through the musical press in June 1894, as an echo of the performance of the *First Symphony*—called at that time *Titan*—on the occasion of the Musicians' Festival of the "Allgemeiner Deutscher Musikverein," in Weimar. To judge by the criticisms, the work had justified indignation by sterility, triviality, and an accumulation of extravagances. It was, above all, the *Funeral March in the Manner of Callot* which was rejected with anger and scorn. I recall distinctly with what excitement I devoured the newspaper reports on the subject. I admired the daring author of so strange a Funeral March and felt a burning desire to know this extravagant man and his extravagant work.

It was but a few months later that a letter of introduction to Pollini, the theatrical manager, took me as coach to the Hamburg Opera, whose first conductor was the same Gustav Mahler. And there he stood in person, in the office of the theater, when I left Pollini's sanctum after my first call upon him: pale, thin, small of stature, with longish features, the steep forehead framed by intensely black hair, remarkable eyes behind spectacles, lines of sorrow and of humor in the face which, when he spoke, would show the most astonishing change of expression—the very incarnation of that Kapellmeister Kreisler—interesting, demoniac, intimidating—as he would appear to the imagination of youthful readers of E. Th. A. Hoffmann's fantastic tales. Pleasantly and kindly he inquired as to my musical ability and knowledge—to which I replied, to his visible satisfaction, with mingled modesty and self-reliance—and left me in a kind of stupor and deep emotion. For my previous experiences, gained in homely surroundings, had taught me that genius was to be met with only in books and musical literature and in the art-treasures of museums, but that living human beings were more or less commonplace and that everyday life was prosaic.

And now I felt as if a higher realm had been opened to me. In his aspect and manner Mahler appeared to me both as a genius and a demon: life itself had all of a sudden become romantic, and I know of nothing that could more aptly characterize the elementary effect of Mahler's personality than the irresistible power with which his entry into a young musician's life brought about a complete change in the latter's views of life.

My next recollection shows him to me at one of the early rehearsals of *Hänsel und Gretel*, a new work then in preparation at the Hamburg Opera. Never before had I seen such an intense person, never dreamed that a terse word, a commanding gesture, and a will directed solely towards a certain goal, could frighten and alarm others and force them into blind obedience. An unsatisfactory piano accompanist tried Mahler's patience; suddenly—what luck!—he saw me, a fascinated onlooker, standing in the wings, and he asked me whether I dared to accompany at sight the opera which was unknown to me. My proud "Why of course!" elicited an amused smile and the request that I should replace the unfortunate colleague who had been removed by a motion of the hand. The often-repeated sung echo in the forest scene was unsatisfactorily shaded; Mahler turned to me with words to this effect: "I trust that you know how things happen in a forest—go and rehearse the echo for me." Thus, one of the very first rehearsals furnished me with a thorough impression of Mahler's manner as a conductor:

guiding and commanding, filled by the work, sure of his goal, irritable and harsh when confronted with an insufficient performance, kind, trusting, sympathetic when he thought he could feel ability and enthusiasm.

The third recollection: Together with Mahler I left the building by the stage door and was about to take leave of him when he detained me with the words: "Come with me for a bit." What I recall of our conversation is merely that I started by making a remark concerning the Humperdinck work which he said was "fashioned in masterly manner, but not really fairy-tale-like." From explaining what fairy-tale-like meant he changed to other subjects, and again I was fascinated to observe how the same intensity, the same spiritual tenseness, that had previously filled his rehearsing was now manifested in his conversation. The vehemence with which he objected whenever I said something that was unsatisfactory to him—and how timidly I said it!—his sudden submersion in pensive silence, the kind glance with which he would receive an understanding word on my part, an unexpected, convulsive expression of secret sorrow and, added to all this, the strange irregularity of his walk: his stamping of the feet, sudden halting and rushing ahead again—everything confirmed and strengthened the impression of demoniac obsession; and I should hardly have been surprised if, after saying good-bye, he had gone faster and faster, and then flown from me finally as a vulture, in the way in which Archivarius Lindhorst left the student Anselmus in Hoffmann's *Golden Pot.*

A fourth recollection completes the initial impressions: following Mahler's invitation to call upon him I entered his study and my first glance was arrested by a reproduction of Giorgione's "Concerto" which hung on the wall. Who is the monk, I asked myself, who, his hands on the keys, seems to have stopped in his playing and turns around? What has he to do with Mahler whom he so strangely resembles? And I recall that, for a long time to come, I mysteriously identified the ascetic monk of the painting with Mahler. As a matter of fact, there is a "family resemblance," but not only to Mahler; every real musician somewhat resembles that monk, although hardly another so closely as did Mahler. The miracle has occurred here that a genius of a painter, with the prophetic anticipation characteristic of genius, has created the musical type; created him and not conceived him from experience; for at the time of Giorgione there was no music yet in our sense of the word; and so the musical type existed even before music itself. The painting furnished the initial subject of our conversation; I have retained no memory as to whether or not there was, at that very first visit, an endeavor on my part to trace the phenomenon of Giorgione's vision; I distinctly recall that we talked about it frequently and I also know that the resemblance to the devout player strengthened my impression of the mysterious element in Mahler's appearance which, in preexistence, seemed to have been portrayed in the fifteenth century. In the course of that visit and the one which followed it I finally succeeded in turning the conversation towards his creative work and in getting him to the piano, and thus the awe-inspiring impression which dominated me was sublimated into a force that stirred up all my faculties of feeling and sympathetic conception, for there was then disclosed to the seeking young musician a magnificent insight into the soul of a creative man. In addition, I was able to participate in the re-creative work of a conductor at home in the very depths of masterpieces and to add to my store of knowledge through the teachings and emotional communications of a universal mind—indeed, it would not have been surprising if, in view of the onrush of great experiences, I had spiritually completely lost my head. That it did not happen I ascribe today to the very fact of my unbounded admiration and devotion: without thought or puzzling, I had made up my mind to follow, to be sympathetic, to collaborate, and since this mental attitude was as natural and congenial to me as Mahler's music and musical activity itself, I fortunately, in spite of all my Mahler worship, did not have to lose my own self. And even if, years later, the unavoidable inner conflict with Mahler's influence led to serious spiritual crises, I am able to confirm what I then felt in my innermost soul: that this influence was a blessing upon my entire life.

Hamburg

I SPENT TWO YEARS IN HAMBURG. A FEW weeks after entering upon my duties, the training of the chorus was entrusted to me at Mahler's instigation, so that in two capacities, both as director of the chorus and as coach, I was able to avail myself of the privilege of collaborating in the performances under the guidance of Mahler, thus becoming familiar directly and actively with his intentions. Very soon I also conducted operas, and when, at the close of my first season, Otto Lohse went to America, I was permitted to shed the snake's skin of chorus-director and coach and don the longed-for and more brilliant garment of the "real" conductor; it goes without saying, however, that I continued as coach of the operas put on by Mahler.

The anxiety of the singers to satisfy Mahler's demands for the utmost both in rhythmical correctness and obedience to dynamic and other precepts communicated itself to me, and led to an intensified exactitude and care in my rehearsals, which were of immeasurable advantage to me later; for my natural inclination was to place emotion in musical activities, dramatics and poetic feeling in delivery, and complete attention to the spiritual contents of the work above musical precision, and to neglect strict accuracy in favor of vitality. Now, however, when rehearsing with Loge or Fricka for Mahler's *Rheingold* presentation, I endeavored most carefully to attain a combination of the most vital expression with that painstaking correctness which Mahler demanded of the singers. How far might I have gone astray in view of my dangerous inclination towards exaggerated sentimentality if I had not learned through Mahler's demands and example how, in the presence of ideal declamation in the works of Wagner, the very fact of rhythmical exactness becomes the surest aid to dramatic expression, and how the co-ordination of the spiritual element with strict musical precepts works altogether to the advantage of a vigorous expression of sentiments!

The *rubato, i.e.* the loosening of the exactness in time and rhythm in favor of holds or accelerations inspired by sentiment, was frequently the subject of exhaustive discussion; even in Italian operatic music, in connection with which Mahler considered a somewhat more accentuated *rubato* an important element of the style, he was against any of the exaggerations which German musicians and singers often advocated. He set the best example of a restrained *rubato*, removed from the arbitrary inclinations of the singer and dictated solely by enthusiasm and passion, in an ever-memorable presentation of *La Traviata*.

In our frequent conversations on the subject of Wagner, my Wagner-frenzy became purified and strengthened through contact with Mahler's Wagnerianism which was inspired by practical experience and deep thought. Thus, my strongest impressions of his activity as a conductor in Hamburg were the *Nibelungen* and *Meistersinger*, to be followed later by his presentation of *Tristan* in Vienna; and the whole of the performances and many details of them will for all time cling to my ear and to my heart. The personality of Wagner, too, furnished an inexhaustible subject of conversation; Mahler never grew tired of defending him against the "Philistines' charge" of ingratitude and disloyalty and, as an explanation of human insufficiencies, of pointing to the fact that the man of genius was wrapped up in his creations. Not only Wagner, however, but every artistic task that happened to present itself became for him a subject for discussion, although never with any intention of exerting an educative influence upon one who was his junior by sixteen years. After all, Mahler was not an educator—he was too much centered in himself, in his work, and in his strongly-agitated inner life, and he gave little thought to other persons and things.

Systematic influence, the most important element of education, was foreign to his wholly ungoverned and impulsive character. Nothing in his life—as I quickly realized—was systematic; his style of living resembled a river with cataracts, like the Nile in its middle course, and not a uniformly flowing stream. In the judgments of his personality, therefore, no epithet appeared even at that time more frequently than the word "desultory." He impressed me, too, as being desultory but not in the sense of a lack of thoroughness—he was ready for the next mental jump only when, in the cataract of thought and feeling, all that had been set in motion had flown forth and come to rest again. To be sure, quiet only lasted until his being effervesced again under a new impulse.

Hardly ever, therefore, did he impart conscious instruction to me, but what I did gain through my living experience of a personality that without premeditation and because of an inner overabundance spent itself freely in word and music, is truly immeasurable. Mahler's impulsive outbursts are a possible explanation of the agitation I was able to notice in almost all the people who came in contact with him. They included those who were nearest to him, but especially, of course, singers and members of the orchestra. He spread about himself an atmosphere of high tension out of which were born performances filled with his intentions and pulsing with the fervor of his enthusiasm which gained for the Hamburg Opera its leading position in the musical life of Germany. While those of higher caliber were attached to him in profound admiration, bitter feeling and hatred issued from the less gifted and arrogant, who felt maltreated by the stern taskmaster. But, willingly or unwillingly, they all bowed to his will.

His inward vitality was at that time the source of a violent outward agility: I can still see him, at an orchestra rehearsal of *Götterdämmerung:* rushing towards the trumpets and trombones in a far corner of the orchestra pit, to impress upon them especially a passage in the *Funeral Music;* or quickly using a double-bass stool to climb up to the stage in order to give directions there, the issuing of which from the conductor's desk would have been less convenient or entailed a loss of time, as, for instance, in connection with the shading of a distant chorus or of music on the stage. The orchestra would, meanwhile, remain in hypnotic silence, under the spell of the master who, himself spellbound by the intrinsic conception of a work of art, seemed urged by a compelling force to make his co-workers comply with the irresistible dictates of his innermost self. At no time during the two years which I spent with Mahler at the Hamburg theater or the six years at the Vienna Opera did I notice a lessening of that high-tension spell. "The magic, too, remained unbroken"[1] at all times and the work was accomplished, from beginning to end, in that rarefied atmosphere which was the element of his life.

The counterpart to such absorbing concentration was bound to be a proportionate absent-mindedness in all things that lay outside the momentary sphere of interest. Many were the comic occurrences resulting from this absent-mindedness. One day, for example, at a stage rehearsal with orchestra, the stage manager asked him to have a little patience because certain matters on the stage needed his immediate attention. Impatient at first, Mahler was soon in deep thought, while the stage manager toiled to put things right. When this was done, however, repeated calls that everything was ready and that he might continue were quite unable to awaken him. Suddenly, aroused by the general quiet and expectation, he looked about in bewilderment, tapped his desk with the baton, and called out: "Zahlen!" (My bill, please!) There were peals of laughter

[1] *Tannhäuser*, Act II, Landgrave to Elizabeth.

from all sides, in which he finally joined heartily himself.

When he had gradually become convinced of my passionate interest in his creative work, it began to give him pleasure to make me familiar with it at the piano. The grotesquely-quaint sounds still linger in my ear as he sang for me *St. Anthony's Sermon to the Fish*, and I recall his high spirits in the rendition of *To make naughty children be good* and *Self-Reliance*, and his passion and sorrow in the *Songs of a Traveling Fellow;* I still feel the deep emotion which shook me when I at last became acquainted through him with the anxiously awaited *First Symphony*. More and more his creative work occupied the foreground of our relations and conversation, and in the study of his works, in our discussions about them and about the books he read, the poets and philosophers he loved, in the ever-deeper view of his soul, my initial impression of Mahler as a fanatic-demoniac nature belonging to the sphere of E. Th. A. Hoffmann broadened into a more correct and inclusive picture, though one more difficult to understand.

Of his astonishing mental range, of the conflicts of his soul, of the dark powers with which he wrestled, of the yearning which was the *leit-motif* of his life and work—of all this I shall speak later. I only want to add here that at that time I sensed or understood of his complicated inner life only as much as my youthful inexperience permitted, but that this vaguely felt understanding nourished in me an increasing admiration for the man, while my growing familiarity with his work deepened my enthusiasm for the musician. How could it have been otherwise when he, usually erratic and eruptive, never met me except in a spirit of kindness, affability, and sympathy?

He was as little inclined regularly to attend operatic performances conducted by me, let alone to supervise my activity, as he was to assume a didactic attitude. On the other hand, he was interested enough in my conducting to attend a performance occasionally and to give me his opinion afterward. At one time, in the last act of a performance of *Aïda* which I conducted, the chorus behind the scene set in about ten measures too soon, probably because the chorus director presumed that an occasionally used cut was to be observed. I succeeded in quickly notifying the orchestra and in "jumping along"; suddenly the chorus stopped and I had to cast about for a new means of saving the situation. But Mahler had jumped up from his seat in a box at the first indication of the mishap and rushed backstage through the connecting corridor to stop the chorus and give the proper cue himself. He could not, of course, have foreseen my quick grasp of the situation. In his immediate and unhesitating intervention, however, all his active concern and impetuosity was so strikingly revealed that the event seems to me worthy of recall.

One of my cherished recollections is our occasional four-handed playing; Schubert's compositions for four hands gave us especially keen pleasure. On such occasions Mahler, who sat at the right, would play with his left hand my upper system so that my right hand naturally had to assume the execution of his lower system, each one of us being therefore obliged continuously to read Primo and Secondo at the same time, a feat which complicated our task amusingly. For some march melodies he invented words which he would sing while playing. He was much addicted to such spontaneous gaiety, and fond, too, of witty aperçus in conversation when he was apt to voice the drollest notions. And yet, immediately after a fit of unrestrained laughter, he would wrap himself in a gloom and silence which nobody dared to disturb.

Irrespective of such sorrow arising from the depths of his being, life furnished enough reasons for the clouding of his soul. His promising younger brother, Otto, of whose musical gifts he thought very highly, shot himself in 1895. Two symphonies were found in his desk, parts of one of which had been performed, while the other had not only failed to meet with a sympathetic response on its performance but had even been ridiculed. There were a number of songs with orchestra, three books of songs with piano accompaniment which, however, nobody ever sang, and a third symphony near its completion.

Mahler's relations with Pollini unavoidably grew worse, as was but natural with characters so different. This was productive of unpleasant incidents in the theater. Mahler was eager to leave Hamburg for the familiar surroundings of Vienna and its incomparable musical atmosphere. At the ring of his door-bell he would often call: "Here comes the summons to the god of the southern zones." But that summons was long in coming; more and more Mahler was in need of a great liberating event, of an important artistic achievement, that would open the way for him. He decided therefore to perform his *Second Symphony* in Berlin with the Philharmonic Orchestra and the Stern Singing Society of that city.

The 13th December 1895, when, for the first time, the entire work was given a hearing—the first three movements had been performed earlier in the year—was a decisive day for Mahler, the composer. The work, of which he himself once wrote: "One is clubbed to the ground, only to be lifted again by angels' wings to the most exalted heights," produced an overwhelming impression at a performance which, according to my recollection, was magnificent. I can still feel the breathless tension with which, after the End of the World in the last movement, the mysterious singing of the bird at the *Great Recall* was listened to, and the general deep emotion at the entry of the chorus *Rise Ye Up, Oh Rise Ye Up*. There were indeed even then adversaries, misconstruction, belittling, scoffing. But the impression of the magnitude and originality of the work, of the power of Mahler's nature, was so profound that the ascent of the composer can justly be dated from that day.

And how badly things might have turned out! Mahler used to suffer at times from headache, the violence of which was in proportion to his vehement nature. His strength would be quite paralyzed. There was nothing for him to do on such occasions but to lie still, as in a swoon. In the year 1900, shortly before a concert with the Vienna Philharmonic Orchestra at the Paris Trocadero, he actually lay thus unconscious for so long that the concert started half an hour late and he was able only with difficulty to lead it to its conclusion. Here in Berlin he had, as a matter of fact, staked his future fate as a composer upon a single card, and there, in the afternoon before the concert, he lay with one of the worst headaches of his life, unable to move or partake of anything. I can still see him as he was that evening before me on the much-too-high, unstable conductor's platform, deathly pale, mastering his affliction, the musicians and singers, and the audience, with a superhuman exertion of his will. For me, too, the day and the victory were of supreme importance. I considered myself thoroughly familiar with the work—I had written not only a four-handed but also a two-handed piano score of it—but when I heard in living sound what I had before experienced only in my soul or in a transposition on the piano, I felt with absolute finality that there lay my life's task. I was made happy by the work, by its triumph, and by my decision to pledge my future energies to Mahler's creations.

Meanwhile, it had become evident that I had got as far as could be expected of so young a man at the Hamburg Stadttheater and could count upon no further advancement there. My relations with Pollini, too, had become strained, and Mahler himself advised me to go to another theater. He had in mind Breslau, where an impending vacancy in the position of second conductor promised a favorable field of activity for me. Upon his recommendation I was engaged by Director Löwe. And so I left Hamburg where the experiences of two years had pointed a way to me which I was solemnly determined to follow.

Steinbach

Early in July 1896 I received from Mahler the following letter which, though it has already been published in his collected letters, may once more be quoted here:

Steinbach am Attersee,
2nd July 1896.

Dear Friend,—Let me reply quite briefly to your greetings and invite you to come here as early as 16th July unless, for reasons unknown to me, you have made other plans for your holidays. My sisters may have informed you that I have not been idle and I hope that, within a few weeks, the entire *Third* will be happily concluded. I am already at the orchestral score, as the first sketch has turned out to be quite clear. I think that the gentlemen of the press, be they appointed or self-appointed, will again have some fits of the staggers, while, on the other hand, those fond of a healthy joke will find that which I have there prepared for them very amusing. The entire thing is unfortunately again tainted with my disreputable sense of humor "and there are plenty of opportunities for indulging my fancy for a fearful racket." At times, too, the musicians play "without the slightest consideration for each other, and all of my rude and brutal nature is shown up in its naked form." That I cannot do without some triviality is sufficiently well known. In this instance, to be sure, it passes all permissible bounds. "One feels, at times, as if one were in a pub or in a stable." Do come quite soon and arm yourself betimes! Your good taste, possibly somewhat purified in Berlin, will again be mightily shocked. Best regards to you and your family, and that we may soon meet again!—Yours as ever,

GUSTAV MAHLER.[1]

The letter showed me in what a happy mood the successful conclusion of the first movement and, consequently, the expectation of an early completion of the *Third Symphony* had put him—the

[1] In this letter, and especially in the passages within quotation marks, Mahler mockingly used the language of some of his harsher critics.

other movements had been composed in 1895—and with great suspense and anticipatory joy I looked forward to the weeks I was to spend with Mahler in Steinbach. It was a splendid day in July when the lake steamer brought me there. Mahler met me at the landing and, in spite of my protest, carried my suitcase down the gangway himself until he was relieved of it by some ministering spirit. When, on our way to his house, my glance fell upon the Höllengebirge, whose forbidding rocky walls formed the background of an otherwise charming landscape, Mahler said: "No need to look there any more—that's all been used up and set to music by me," and he immediately began to speak of the construction of the first movement, the introduction of which bore the tentative title: *Was mir das Felsgebirg erzählt.* My impatience to become acquainted with the *Third* had, however, to be curbed for a time. He could never throughout his life be induced to play or show a single note of a work which was not entirely completed. Otherwise, however, I found Mahler in Steinbach more confiding than I had ever known him. Here, in the quiet of nature, untroubled by operatic cares, occupied only by his creative impulse and his thoughts, he was completely himself, and all the riches of his soul were poured out upon those around him.

On the meadow, between the lake and the inn where he had taken lodgings, he had had four walls and a roof erected. In this ivy-clad "Composer's Cottage," whose furniture consisted of a piano, table, chairs and sofa and the opening of whose door would cause a shower of beetles to descend upon the person coming in, he spent his mornings in work, undisturbed by the noises of the house and the road. He went there at six in the morning, at seven his breakfast was silently placed before him, and only when he opened his door would he return to normal life. According to schedule, that should have occurred at twelve o'clock, but sometimes it was three before the hungry members of the household and the cook fussing about her dishes were relieved of their wait. Not all of that time, however, was spent in his Composer's Cottage; he would stroll about in the meadow, climb the hills, or take longer walks, but he always returned to "put the crop into the barn." In high spirits he would then join the common noon-day meal which passed in lively conversation. He was apt to derive pleasure from a well-cooked dish and to show special gratification when some tasty sweets had been prepared. It was up to the inventive faculty of the cook, he declared, to surprise him for four weeks with a daily change of sweets. In the afternoon, we took walks together or made music; in the evening, we chatted or read, and frequently Mahler would interrupt the general quiet to read a passage which seemed to him worthy of being repeated. As far as I remember, it was his pleasure in Cervantes' *Don Quixote* which he could not keep to himself, and I vividly recall how laughter prevented him from going on with his reading when he came to the fight with the windmills. But no matter how much amused he was at the deeds and speeches of master and servant, his compassion for the idealism and purity of *Don Quixote* outweighed all other feelings, and he declared that he was always deeply moved when he put the book away.

He derived real pleasure from two young kittens whose antics he never grew tired of watching. He used to take them with him on short walks in his roomy coat pockets to enjoy their company when resting. The little animals had become so used to him that they would even play hide-and-seek with him, a fact of which he was not a little proud. Dogs, cats, birds, and the animals of the forest amused him and excited his most serious interest. He endeavored by careful watching to fathom their nature and, in the woods, he responded to the hopping or song of a bird, or to the jumping of a squirrel, with an involuntary exclamation of pleasure and sympathy. He told me he could never forget how once, at night in the country, the mournful lowing of the cattle had pained him deeply, for it impressed him as the sentient sound from the stolid soul of the beast.

Our summer in Steinbach passed in a quiet, even tenor, a condition essential to Mahler's creative work, for the actual composing had to be completed during the holidays if he were to return to the city with a finished sketch of the orchestral score. The final instrumentation and its last polish could be reserved for the winter; inspiration and creative processes were incompatible with Mahler's activity as a conductor. Finally, towards the end of the summer, came the day on which Mahler was able to play to me the finished *Third*. Through our conversations, which had been filled with the aftereffects of his morning ecstasies, I knew the spiritual atmosphere of the symphony long before its musical contents. Nevertheless it was, for the musician in me, an undreamed-of and revolutionizing event when he played the work for me on the piano. The force and novelty of the musical language fairly stunned me, and I was overwhelmed to feel in his playing the same creative fervor and exaltation which had given birth to the work itself. It seemed to me that only then, and only through that music, I had fully recognized him. His entire being seemed to breathe a mysterious affinity with nature; how deep, how elemental it was I had only been able to feel intuitively, and now I had learned it directly from the musical language of his symphonic world dream. If he had been a "nature lover" in the usual sense of the word —let us say a garden enthusiast—his music, I thought, would have turned out to be more "civilized." But what I had always felt subconsciously—his Dionysian saturation with nature—was voiced here as a primitive musical sound from the very depths of his soul. It seemed to me that I could see him through and through: could see the oppressive weight upon his soul placed there by the forbidding majesty of the rocky summits, could see his love of the tender flower, could see how in primeval depths of darkness he entered into the feelings of the beasts of the forest, whose joys and animation, whose shyness and drollery, whose cruelty and ferocity, had inspired the third movement—I saw him and I saw Pan within him. At the same time, however, I felt in him the yearning human being who, with intuitive foresight, had penetrated beyond the boundaries of mundane transience and of whom the last three movements tell their tale. Thus light was thrown by him upon his work and was reflected back upon him by the work.

The beautiful summer was drawing to its close and the unwanted approach of the next operatic season in Hamburg cast its shadows upon Mahler's moods. Again he would sigh with redoubled yearning for the "summons to the god of the southern zones." I parted from him, but I carried the music of the *Third* within me and it was long before its exciting presence had turned into a soothed possession.

. . . . . .

An infrequent but regular correspondence served to keep up our relationship during the ensuing five years when I was active successively at the theaters of Breslau, Pressburg, Riga and, finally, at the Royal Opera-house in Berlin. When, towards the end of my Breslau contract, no other engagement was in sight and it seemed to me that my year's military service was the best use I could make of a time which otherwise might pass uselessly, Mahler, without hesitation, wrote to put at my disposal the money which I lacked for that year. Fortunately, I had no need to accept his sacrifice—for such it would have been—since at the last moment the Pressburg position was offered me and with it, to my unspeakable joy, the opportunity for frequent visits to Vienna, not far distant, where I would be able to see Mahler again and witness important revivals of operas under his guidance at the Hofoper.

In the meantime, the longed-for had happened: the "summons" had come. On the 11th May 1897 Mahler had appeared for the first time at the conductor's desk of the Wiener Hofoper, his presentation, on that occasion, of *Lohengrin* having created an effect of something elemental. In the autumn of the same year he was made managing director. What a splendid experience it was for me again to meet the man, whom I recalled in connection with so many phases of informal summer life on the Attersee, as the ruler of the world's most brilliant Opera; to step from the small Pressburg theater, where I was acting as "First Kapellmeister," with its modest artistic resources, with beginners on the stage and a simple audience in the auditorium, into the splendors of the Wiener Hofoper: the Philharmonists in the orchestra pit; on the stage, in addition to the reigning favorites, talented artists discovered by Mahler; a festive audience in a magnificent house—and Mahler at the desk. Thus I enjoyed the never-to-be-forgotten performances of *Dalibor*, *Djamileh*, *Eugen Onegin*, *Flying Dutchman*, and others, and Mahler's example protected me from the danger of becoming too thoroughly accustomed to the insufficiencies of my own sphere of work.

My visits to Vienna provided the opportunity for renewed contact with Mahler, inclusion in the circle of his Vienna friends, and the enjoyment of the mental stimulation that emanated from him and which, during the year in Breslau, I had so greatly missed.

Pressburg was followed, in my career, by distant Riga, whence I was able, for two years, to keep in touch with Mahler only by correspondence. During that time a misunderstanding arose between us which, fortunately, has remained the only one. In October 1898 Mahler offered me a conductor's position at the Vienna Opera, for 1900, *i.e.* after the expiration of my Riga contract, and added that he would like me to obtain my release as early as the autumn of 1899. This caused me an internal conflict: I felt drawn to Vienna and Mahler, and his remark about the importance of obtaining my services before 1900, since, if he had to continue work under the then prevailing conditions, he would be dead by that time, was a moral pressure on my soul. On the other hand, I, a young man of twenty-two, felt my own powers growing and my independence developing in the work and responsibility of First Conductor at a comparatively good theater like the Riga Opera, and I hesitated to place myself then under the guidance of Mahler and—a thought which had never up to that time occurred to me—to run the risk of jeopardizing my own self-development. I wrote to him in that sense, but he, unwilling to entertain my scruples, felt disappointed in me as one who had deserted him in his time of need, and so there arose between us a misunderstanding which I felt very keenly. Nevertheless, I believed that I ought to stick to my decision, and when, in the course of the following year, I received an offer from the Berlin Opera, for 1900, I accepted, though not without having informed Mahler and again explained the reasons for my refusal of the year before. He replied kindly and in a conciliatory spirit and held out the hope that the unpleasant episode belonged to the past.

So I went to Berlin where, after several months of activity, I received another summons from Mahler. There was then no hesitation or doubt for me; I managed to obtain my release from my Berlin duties at the expiration of the first year of my contract and, in the autumn of 1901, full of hope and happiness, I entered upon my work at the Wiener Hofoper.

Vienna

It is difficult to speak of the Mahler epoch at the Vienna Opera in the subdued accents of recollection; rather should one extol it in exalted language as a ten year feast to which a great artist invited co-workers and devotees. What a stroke of good fortune in the history of our art that the rich resources of a noble institute of art were, for a decade, placed at the disposal of a musical genius, a man of force, passionately devoted to the stage; and that this period of activity coincided with the prime of his life and, at the same time, with a period of comparative political quiet.

Mahler was now indeed at the zenith of his life. During these ten years, the fires of his soul burned with an ever purer glow, his powers derived new vigor from the lavishness with which he expended them and from the artistic accomplishments to whose importance his own instinct and public acclaim bore witness. And there was no end to giving.

When I entered upon my duties as a conductor in Vienna, Mahler had already been active at the Hofoper for four years. But his every appearance in the orchestra pit was preceded by the tenseness with which one looks forward to a sensation. The house grew silent when, with quick, firm steps, he made for the desk. If a whisper should arise or an embarrassed late-comer sneak in, Mahler would turn round and a dead silence reign over the intimidated audience. He would begin—and everybody was under his spell. Before the opening of the third act, he was invariably received with a hurricane of applause which made it difficult for him to resume. That was the order of things throughout the period of his incumbency.

Just as, at his first appearance at the Opera's desk, he had taken Vienna by storm, so he retained his dominion over the souls of his audience to the very last performance, and no hostility aimed at the director of the Opera, no fight waged against the composer, was capable of ousting him from his position. His popularity in a city which had a veritable passion for the theater and for music was quite extraordinary. When he crossed the street, hat in hand and gnawing his lip or the inside of his cheek, even the drivers of the cabs would turn their heads after him and whisper to each other in awe: "Der Mahler!" To be popular is not tantamount, however, to being beloved, and no one can say that he was the "Darling of Vienna." The easy-going thought him far too exacting. In the Phaeacian Vienna of pre-War days, this singularly unobliging and implacably fierce man exerted an intimidating fascination upon the public at large and upon those with whom he came more intimately in contact. At any rate, the Viennese thought him highly interesting; that he abolished the claque, did away with all cuts in the works of Wagner—an Herculean deed in those days!—refused to grant leaves of absence to the artists, treated old-time favorites among the singers brusquely: all these things were discussed eagerly in Vienna. His bearish actions furnished a favorite topic of coffee-house gossip and his caustic repartee was widely circulated. He had a special gift for impressively formulating his words. When, in his presence, I once explained to a Tristan the change in attitude and expression the love potion was meant to produce, pointing out that restraint and reserve would have to be abandoned entirely and that the change must extend even to vocal expression, Mahler interrupted me by saying: "My dear S., don't forget: before the potion you are a baritone, after it a tenor." An influential person recommended to him a new opera, suggesting the possibility that the composer, who up to that time had not been signally successful, might have produced something after all that was really beautiful. Mahler replied courteously: "Nothing is impossible, but it is improbable that an orange should grow on a chestnut tree."

He told me that he felt instinctively impelled to be drastic in talk because experience had taught him that he could thus make himself understood most quickly and impressively. He added, laughing, that for his purpose this practical advantage was more important than exactness of thought, in which, in almost every instance, quick repartee was lacking. The public at large was intensely interested in these remarks of Mahler, and I recall that a journalist, the editor of *Sunday Chats,* implored me by telephone on a number of occasions to tell him Mahler's latest original remark—his public demanded to know it.

His first years in Vienna passed in overwhelming achievements on his part and enthusiastic and personal interest on the part of the artistic public. Essentially, it was still the same atmosphere of exalted giving and taking which I found when I first took up my work. It made Mahler happy to be able to produce such magnificent performances of beloved works with the rich resources of the Hofoper and for its music-loving audiences; and the latter themselves always seemed to be in festive mood. It is true that, even prior to my coming, he had, as conductor of the Philharmonic concerts, caused storms of protest by his retouchings of the instrumentation of the *Ninth* and by using a full string orchestra to perform Beethoven's *String Quartet in F Minor*, but I witnessed only the last dying sounds, as it were, of that combat. Incomparable operatic performances, like that of the *Tales of Hoffmann*—a veritable model of imaginative dramatic exhaustion of a work and of inspired musicianship—had aroused the entire musical Vienna to a high pitch of enthusiasm and been the means of re-establishing amicable relations. It was his personal policy that cast a gloom upon the atmosphere once more. He succeeded in securing the services of important young artists; but when he made them the main supports of his glorious performances, every dimming of the luster of old stars by the rising younger ones caused offense and ill-feeling which, at times, assumed considerable proportions.

Mahler's endeavors on behalf of the young generation of singers made the public uneasy for another and more weighty reason. He had, from the very beginning, with the confidence and interest characteristic of the optimist, shown a liking for what was new. Faithfully productive artistic endeavor and scepticism are incompatible. Every new voice, every new talent, meant to him high expectations and even confident hope. When new voices were tried on the stage he would listen hopefully and without prejudice, always ready to be surprised by a newly discovered gift, and hurt by the more critical attitude of those around him. Naturally, all of Mahler's hopes for new singing sensations implied guest appearances, which burdened the repertoire and endangered the performances, inasmuch as important parts had to be entrusted to guest artists who frequently were unable, when actually appearing before the public in an exacting part, to justify the high expectations which an initial hearing had prompted. Mahler's impulsive enthusiasm was then likely to change, with the full vehemence of his nature, to violent rejection; but none of these experiences was able to cure his optimism.

In retrospect, however, it becomes clear what a lucky hand Mahler had during his incumbency in the engaging of leading artists and that the importance of his finds justified his continual searches. I need not mention by name the artists whose services he secured, for their accomplishments will forever be inscribed in the glorious annals of the Vienna Opera.

His inclination, when casting a part, to consider less the voice of the artist than his personality was interesting to me, though the public viewed it with grave misgivings. Thus—to quote the most striking example of a maxim which, as a rule, he practised chiefly in connection with "small parts"—he once allotted the bass part of Kaspar in *Freischütz* to a baritone who had a rather extraordinary aptitude for portraying sinister characters, because among the bassos, in spite of eminent vocal qualifications, there was not a man who could do justice to the embodiment of that gloomy figure. He never hesitated, when it seemed imperative, to subordinate the musical to the dramatic point of view.

Mahler's repertoire and his choice of novelties and revivals displayed his cultivation of the recognized, resurrection of the wrongfully neglected, and love for the new. The full scope of his nature becomes apparent in the composite picture of the operas of all kinds and styles which he recalled to flourishing life—from Gluck to Mozart and down to Pfitzner and Charpentier. One reason why his repertoire produced the effect of rich variety was that it contained and continued to contain works not yet generally popular, whose merits only his fine formative skill had been able to disclose, as, for instance, Boieldieu's *White Lady*, Goetz's *The Taming of the Shrew*, Halevy's *The Jewess*, and many others.

While thus his repertoire caused little dissatisfaction, it was different when his serious mind turned to new problems. What is today recognized and appreciated as pioneer work on the part of Mahler, was then but in the nature of an experiment and caused excitement and strife. I have in mind his collaborations with Alfred Roller, the productions of *Tristan, Fidelio, Walküre, Don Giovanni, Magic Flute, Iphigenia*—as many revivals as they were stages of progress on a road blocked for him by operatic problems of style which he recognized with ever-increasing clarity. I shall content myself here with this allusion because, later, I propose to speak connectedly on the subject of the director's and conductor's work.

Concerning the general public's attitude towards Mahler's activity during his last years in Vienna it may be said that, while the best remained his followers to the very day of his departure, admiring the daring spirit that penetrated beyond accepted theories into the realm of the problematic and approving the ruthless vehemence with which he pursued his artistic goals, his fanaticism, on the other hand, and the personal harshness of his expressions brought him many enemies amongst the more commonplace and faint-hearted of his co-workers, while his dauntlessness in the domain of art aroused the antagonism of the more conservative element among the public and press. They looked with disfavor upon the uncomfortably new and did not realize that the experiment of today created the law of tomorrow.

While, however, Mahler actually owed their enmity only to the daring magnitude of his achievement—important innovations invariably being subject to attack—it must be admitted that, in the case of personal ill-feeling, he was frequently the innocently guilty party. The increasing harshness of his character has its explanation in his reaction to the Viennese "softness" of that period and signified a kind of adaptation with reversed signature. Through the fascination exercised by the thrilling conductor and the dynamic man he had at the outset asserted himself irresistibly. To hold this ground in the face of a world inclined to relax existing tensions relentlessness was necessary. But since his way as a seeker did not run smoothly but led to ever new heights, far from the beaten track, his artistic demands continued to increase and became more and more complicated. With all of his kindness and depth of feeling, Mahler's was a "masterful mind," endowed with a gift for commanding to which, at the K.k. Hofoperntheater [1] with its consciousness of a glorious past, people were not accustomed. The genius loci of the magnificent house, with the splendor of its artistic resources,

[1] Kaiserlich-königliches Hofoperntheater: Imperial and Royal Opera-house.

had, before Mahler's advent, rather resembled the worldly youth in Giorgione's "Concerto" than the lofty-minded and serious monk at the manual. The latter's spirit, however, had made its entry into the Opera with Mahler's coming and strove to place its seal upon an institution which theretofore had sought its justification in the splendor of voices, in a sensuously beautiful production of music, and in the luxury of its stage settings. The views and demands, therefore, which had their logical foundation in Mahler's nature, in his spiritual attitude towards art, in his relation to the masterworks of operatic literature and, above all, in his downright earnestness, were bound to be a new and exciting element in the cultural atmosphere of the sensual and epicurean city.

When, in the first year of his directorship, he was received in audience by Emperor Franz Joseph, the latter praised him for having succeeded in "making himself the master of conditions at the Opera." It was Mahler's task to retain this mastery if he wanted to realize his artistic aims. In this he succeeded in spite of the fact that his aims became ever higher, his demands severer and, consequently, his methods harsher. The rigor of his manner, however, was hardly ever directed against the truly gifted or the earnestly striving artist. He was patient in the face of their insufficiencies and gave them evidence of both his musical and his personal appreciation. A highly gifted singer, and one he liked very much, was in the habit of always making the same mistake at a certain place in a Mozart opera. During a performance of that work a short-circuit caused some smoke to appear on the stage. The audience became uneasy, and a panic was only prevented by Mahler's presence of mind, the words of reassurance he shouted to the audience, and the self-possession of that very singer who continued in his part as if nothing untoward had happened. After the performance, Mahler patted him on the shoulder and said laughingly: "I believe, my dear X., there has to be a fire before you can sing that passage correctly."

In contrast with the amiable spirit of that censure is the following example of ruthless severity. At one of the last rehearsals, or maybe it was even at the final one, of a new production he was not at all satisfied with the singer of the leading part, a very famous and popular artist. Mahler voiced his dissatisfaction forcibly from his desk, relieved the singer of his part and offended him publicly by choosing someone else to sing in his place at the first performance.

How kind and considerate he could be at times was shown in his attitude towards a member of the Opera who was hopelessly ill; his assiduous efforts on his behalf succeeded in procuring for him easier duties, financial relief, and even a new contract, by which he meant to allay the artist's anxiety and to deceive him concerning the hopelessness of his condition. There were, in that instance, no artistic considerations to be dealt with; but when there were he would be quite intransigeant and could not understand why he should be expected to use milder means. When I once spoke to him about this or some similar occurrence and tried to convince him that undue harshness could be avoided, he made the memorable and truly naïve reply: "Well, what do you want, am I not always quickly reconciled?" It was impossible to make it clear to him that it was the other fellow who had cause to be irreconciled, the weaker nature being unable to distinguish clearly between the humane and artistic aspects.

In a beautiful farewell letter to the members of the Opera he wrote that "in the press of battle and in the heat of the moment neither you nor I have been spared wounds and misunderstandings." Big issues had been at stake, however, and how significant and complete the victory was can, indeed, be realized only today when the Mahler epoch and the accompanying achievements of its artists have assumed legendary importance.

Then, again, Mahler was more ruthless with himself than with anybody else. He demanded the utmost of himself at every rehearsal and, even at times of physical indisposition, he knew no consideration. It is almost unbelievable that he should have written the *Fourth*, *Fifth*, *Sixth*, *Seventh* and *Eighth Symphonies*, in addition to a number of songs with orchestra, during the short holiday periods in the course of his directorship, and that, in other words, for ten years the enormous task of managing an Opera had had its only relief in the even more tremendous one of creative work. His life seemed to be an ever-recurring orbit of strength: he lavished it upon art and, renewed, he seemed to recover it from art. During the entire period of his incumbency in Vienna, with the exception of the last year, I never saw him other than brisk, inspired, and charged with energy.

It has to be considered, too, that his work-day began as a rule quite early in the morning at home, when the instrumentation of his last work would keep him at his desk for an hour or two. He would then walk to the Opera, where he attended to correspondence and business details until it was time to rehearse. At noon we frequently went out together and, usually by a detour through the Stadtpark, I walked with him as far as his flat in Auenbruggerstrasse. Occasionally there were afternoon meetings at a coffee-house and infinitely stimulating evenings at his home or with friends. Never to be forgotten are the evenings at the restaurant after one of his great premières when, the task being accomplished, he liked to talk comprehensively about the work that had just been produced. His conversation, both stimulating and stimulated, found ever new nourishment in the surging wealth of his thinking and feeling. Nevertheless, I seem to recall that, in Vienna—due to the closer contact with the demands of the day brought about by his position and responsibility—he did not, on the whole, permit his thoughts to soar so much or to be so fully immersed in transcendental matters; mundane affairs had a larger share in them. And yet, his utterances in connection with questions of the day showed the distant and superior attitude of the artist whose home is not in the world but in his art, of the man who carries his loneliness with him. Frequently, too, metaphysical questions would suddenly spring up in his heart and in his conversation—that *basso ostinato* of his spiritual life which at times might be blotted out but never discontinued. Every contact with his creative work, be it through his morning work at his desk or through the performances of his compositions in Vienna or elsewhere, would divert his gaze from the wealth of daily affairs to his own heart.

The *Fourth Symphony*, which had been begun in the summer of 1899, was completed in 1900. In

December 1901 it had its first performance in Munich and was vigorously denounced. I was not there and only learned from a friend of the ungracious reception. Very plainly do I recall the first Vienna performance of the *Fourth*, in 1902, when contrasting opinions clashed so violently that enthusiasts and adversaries almost came to blows over it.

In Vienna Mahler's creations were able to gain ground but slowly. The musical public which followed the operatic conductor almost unconditionally were, for many years, preponderantly in opposition to the composer. It was the year 1902 which was to bring him his life's most decisive success as a composer through the victorious performance of his *Third Symphony* at a Musical Festival in Krefeld, the victory being an enduring one. From that time, other conductors began to take an interest in his works and he joined the ranks of the "performed" composers. The Cologne première of his *Fifth*, in 1904, I recall vividly for a special reason: it was the first and, I believe, the only time that the performance of one of Mahler's works under his own guidance left me unsatisfied. The instrumentation did not clearly bring out the contrapuntal structure of the voices, and Mahler himself complained to me afterwards that he seemingly would, after all, never be able to attain mastership in the treatment of the orchestra. It is a fact that he subsequently subjected the instrumentation to the most thorough revision he had ever felt induced to undertake. The reception accorded to the symphony was, as far as I recall, very enthusiastic and plainly showed the growth of the composer's general importance.

Mahler's own attitude towards manifestations of either displeasure or approval was one of stoical calm. The stormy performance of his *Fourth* in Vienna had hardly been able to put him out of humor and, while the victory of his *Third* had pleased him, he had remained entirely free from the intoxication of success. It was all the more affecting, then, to see him depressed almost to tears after the world première of his *Sixth*, the *Tragic Symphony*, as he called it, by the disparaging remarks of a very important musician. I do not recall any other similar experience in connection with him and I am sure that this extraordinary sensitiveness was considerably influenced by the violent emotion his own gloomy work had called forth. He seemed almost impervious to praise or censure on the part of the critics. On the morning after the performance of one of his own works or of an important operatic production he was in the habit of asking sarcastically: "Well, what do the honorable chiefs have to say?" and he always received the reports with equanimity.

One of my fond memories is of a concert which the "Society of Creative Musicians," of which I was then a member, had invited Mahler to conduct. To the deep reverence in which he was held by the young composers, Schönberg and Zemlinsky at their head, Mahler responded with hearty sympathy. Thus the evening, in the course of which only songs with orchestra were performed, was turned into a veritable Mahler celebration. I believe it took place in the Small Hall of the Musikverein, the performers being some excellent singers from the Opera and a chamber orchestra composed of Philharmonic artists led by Mahler.

On that evening Mahler was really happy. In the young musicians' undoubted devotion, more beautiful and pleasing to him than the loud acclaim of the great public, he felt the response of the heart to the call of his own heart in his songs. Every one of these striving and talented followers received, when they occasionally met Mahler, only impressions of sympathy, of interest, and of ungrudging kindness. It is a fact that, in personal intercourse, talent and an exalted striving were the key to Mahler's heart. I doubt if any gifted and high-minded person ever was treated gruffly by him. To be sure, a man with his essential naturalness could never feel at home in so-called "society." He always held himself aloof from its conventions, its conversation, and its formalities, while he felt attracted by high intellect, by originality, and by sincerity. Thus he formed an intimidating element in a society which, as a matter of fact, he sought out but rarely and, usually, reluctantly. If he was in high spirits and in a talkative mood there were smiling faces all about. His ill-humor, on the other hand, spread itself like a thunder-cloud over the minds of all, and only he himself could banish the distress.

While, on the one hand, he was very obliging, sympathetic, and ready to help, he was capable, on the other, of unparalleled rudeness. Once when we left the Opera at noon-time, we were joined by a musician who, generally speaking, was quite agreeable but whose presence was not welcome to Mahler at the moment. In the middle of a conversation he himself had started, Mahler suddenly, without a word of explanation or leave-taking, ran after a tram-car, and was carried away. It was an instinctive flight from a conversation which, at the moment, was undesirable, and he was surely quite unconscious of having been impolite.

On a hot June day, a composer played his opera for him. I joined them towards the end of the last act and found both in their shirt-sleeves, the composer perspiring profusely and Mahler obviously sunk in the depths of boredom and aversion. When the playing had ended, Mahler did not utter a word. The composer, too, probably deeply hurt by Mahler's silence, said nothing, and I saw no chance of saving the awkward situation by any effort of my own. There was no help for it: the composer put on his coat, wrapped up his score and, after a silence that lasted for several minutes, a coldly polite "Auf Wiedersehen!" terminated the painful scene. An entire lifetime of personal relations of all kinds had not supplied Mahler with that modicum of social polish which would have brought the meeting to an ordinary end.

On the other hand, if he was sympathetically impressed, he was by no means lacking in courtesy and kindness, while his bearing produced the undoubted effect of elegance and good breeding. And he had "backbone," no matter whether he was in familiar surroundings, before the public, or facing his superiors in office. It is to the latter's credit that they had sufficient respect for a great artist and a self-willed character to support him even in rather critical instances. What could be more natural, however—inasmuch as Mahler's adversaries were forever trying to influence both the press and the highest officials—than that, towards the end of the ten years, the ground was thoroughly undermined?

The final reason for his resignation, the exact nature of which I do not recall, was only the drop which causes a full vessel to overflow. Shortly prior to it, Mahler, in his drastic manner, described the situation to me by saying, while tilting the legs of a chair: "You see, that's what they are now doing to me: if I wanted to remain seated, all I would have to do is to lean back firmly and I could hold my own. But I am not offering any resistance, and so I shall finally slide off."

Soon afterwards, Mahler summoned me at noon from a rehearsal and together we left the building. I can see him now walking down the Ringstrasse at my side while, in quiet and mild accents, he informed me of his resignation. His words still sound in my ear: "In the ten years at the Opera I have completed my circle."

And, in a profound sense, he was right: his labor for the Opera and its work of art was finished. Now it had to yield, to make room in his inmost self for his last great creations. I recall that we spoke of his future, of his proposed activity in America, the proceeds of which were to ensure certain comforts of life, of a quieter mode of living, and so forth. When I got home, still under the influence of his news, I wrote him a serious letter to which he replied in a few very beautiful lines.

How much graver, however, and how much more

deeply moving was the news which he gave me in the autumn of the same year, again in the course of a walk on the Ringstrasse: he informed me of a heart affection which his physician had suddenly discovered. It recalled to me an incident at a *Lohengrin* rehearsal which had made me uneasy at the time. Delivery and acting in the swan-chorus did not seem to him vivacious enough. To give the chorus an example, he grasped the hands of two men of the chorus at the place: *A miracle!* and, with an expression of the most exalted excitement, he pulled them half-way across the stage towards King Henry. How often had he not in like manner inspired the chorus to unheard-of performances! On that occasion, he suddenly let go of the two men and stopped, motionless and deathly pale, hand pressed to his heart. I presume that at that moment he had, for the first time, felt the insufficiency of his heart.

Now he spoke to me of the serious consequences which the discovery of his ailment would have for him and of the revolutionary changes necessary in his mode of living and creating. He who had at all times been wont to listen to his musical inspiration on long walks, and even while climbing mountains, was now condemned to a most careful reserve in physical exertion. This meant to him not only a grievous deprivation but also fear for his creative work.

More important, however, than the certainly serious changes in his mode of working seemed to me his altered outlook upon life. Death, towards whose mysteries his thought and perception had so often taken their flight, had suddenly come in sight. The world and life now lay in the sinister shadow of its nearness. While, at the time, we spoke quite unsentimentally and to the point, there was no mistaking the darkness which had settled over his entire being.

"Well, I'll get used to it," he said, and how brave and successful was his endeavor is shown by the birth of *Das Lied von der Erde* and the *Ninth Symphony* after he had been taken ill.

In October 1907 he parted from the Hofoper with a performance of *Fidelio* and, in November, with a presentation of his *Second,* he said farewell to his Vienna friends whose expressions of love, loyalty and sorrow, occasioned by the news of his leaving, had deeply pleased and moved him.

A great epoch of operatic art had come to an end —the achievement of one man and of his inspired co-workers. Everyone had learned from him, everyone had been led to the utmost of his capacity. The achievements of his art are looked upon today as the unforgotten days of glory of the Vienna Opera, and the pure will to art that carried it to such heights will ever remain a shining example.

Last Years

IN DECEMBER 1907 MAHLER WENT TO THE United States for the first time. Hundreds had assembled at the station at an early morning hour to bid him farewell upon his leaving Vienna. Strenuous though the activity was which awaited him, he nevertheless felt greatly relieved at first when looking back upon the ten years of work and responsibility as the director of the Vienna Opera, and all the more so since, at the Metropolitan Opera, he was not asked to solve any new problems, but only to produce, with the New York resources, works with which he was familiar. While his concert activity, 1909–1910 and 1910–1911, again brought in its wake grave responsibilities and made considerable demands upon his working strength, it only covered the period of half a year at a time.

During the last years of his life I saw Mahler but

rarely. Measured by the almost uninterrupted contact of the preceding six years, the few weeks he spent in Vienna between a winter's conducting in New York and a summer's work in Toblach, the days of the world première of his *Seventh* in Prague, that of the *Eighth* in Munich and, finally, the hours of our last meeting in Paris, represented a scant space of time. Let me recall first the beautiful autumn days in Prague where many experiences from the time he spent at the Landestheater as a young conductor awoke in him and became the subject of conversation, and where, above all, the rehearsals and performance of the *Seventh Symphony* furnished occasions for a most vivid interchange of thoughts. Mahler was quite satisfied with the instrumentation and we were able to say definitely that every measure was perfected. There was a motor tour into the beautiful surroundings, conversations between us two alone or in the presence of his family and friends, and a spirit of heartfelt harmony prevailed.

In the winter, 1909–1910, Emil Gutmann, the concert manager, prepared the way for a production of the *Eighth Symphony* to which Mahler at first looked forward uneasily. He called the undertaking, which unknown to him was advertised by Gutmann as the *Performance of the Symphony of a Thousand*, the "Barnum and Bailey Exhibition," and foresaw inadequacies and difficulties of organization in the preparations necessitating the use of large numbers of people. At his request, I had selected the soloists and coached them. When he came to Vienna, in the spring of 1910, he attended a rehearsal with piano at my home. A terrible thunderstorm broke as we began and compelled us every little while to interrupt the rehearsal. The heavenly sabotage of our work failed, however, to arouse his impatience and he received the performances of the soloists with a gentle expression of pleasure. I noticed that the gentleness of him who once was feared by all made a strangely moving impression upon those present. He subsequently went to Toblach,[1] his mind at ease concerning the rehearsing of the choruses, and came to Munich early in September.

Those were great days for us who were privileged to attend the rehearsals of the *Eighth*. The immense apparatus obeyed with devotion the master's effortless direction. All performers were in a state of solemn exaltation, and this was true, above all, of the children, whose hearts he had captured from the beginning. It was a great moment when, greeted by the thousands who filled the giant exhibition hall, he took his place facing the thousand performers—

[1] A summer resort, then in the Austrian Tyrol, now belonging to Italy and called Dobiacco.

at the zenith of his life and yet marked by fate for an early death—when his music invoked the creator spiritus by whose fires it had been generated within him, and when from all lips burst forth the yearning call of his life: *Ascende lumen sensibus, infunde amorem cordibus!* When the last note of the performance had died away and the waves of enthusiastic applause reached him, Mahler ascended the steps of the platform, at the top of which the children's choir was posted. The little ones hailed him with shouts of jubilation and, walking down the line, he pressed every one of the little hands that were extended towards him. The loving greeting of the young generation filled him with hope for the future of his work and gave him sincere pleasure. Occasional indications of physical weariness in the course of the rehearsals had made his friends uneasy. At the performance itself he seemed to be at the height of his power—the uplifting of his soul once more had given back to the tired heart its one-time vigor. But it was the last performance of one of his own creations that he himself conducted. He never heard the actual sounds of the two following works.

When he spoke to me of *Das Lied von der Erde* for the first time, he called it a *Symphony in Songs.* It was to have been his *Ninth.* Subsequently, however, he changed his mind. He thought of Beethoven and Bruckner, whose *Ninth* had marked the ultimate of their creation and life, and did not care to challenge fate. He turned the manuscript over to me for study, and it was the first time that it was not he himself who introduced me to a new work. When I brought it back to him, almost unable to utter a word, he turned to the *Abschied* and said: "What do you think? Is this to be endured at all? Will not people make away with themselves after hearing it?" Then he pointed out the rhythmical difficulties and asked jestingly: "Have you any idea how this is to be conducted? I haven't."

The orchestral score of the *Ninth*—inasmuch as it was a symphony the ominous designation of *Ninth Symphony* could no longer be avoided—was, I believe, not even handed to me by himself. I see from one of his letters that he had taken it with him to New York in the autumn of 1909 "in an almost illegible condition," and that he had made a fair copy of it there during his concert activity. He probably brought it back to Vienna in the spring of 1910, but I cannot recall having seen it at the time and it is likely that it came to me only after his death. Perhaps, too, he was prevented by the superstitious awe, which I have already mentioned, from telling me of the fact that, after all, a *Ninth* had come into existence. Up to that time, I had never noticed even a trace of superstition in his clear, strong spirit. And even on that occasion it turned out to be not that but an only-too-well-founded foreboding of the terrible consistency of the Parcae.

The briefness of my meetings with Mahler during the last years of his life is compensated in my recollection of them by the intensity of what he had to say and the weightiness of experience with which every one of our conversations was fraught. Just as in nature twilight is followed by the brightness of the sunset glow, so the world, after the initial darkening of his vitality through his ailment, lay now before him in the mild light of farewell. The "dear Earth" whose song he had written looked so beautiful to him in that light that everything he thought or uttered was mysteriously permeated with a feeling of surprise at the new charm of the old life. I shall never be able to forget his expression when he told me how, on the occasion of a country visit in Moravia, he had found the world to be more beautiful than ever before and what a peculiarly fervent happiness he had derived from the smell of the soil arising from the fields. In the background of his conversation there was now a constant spiritual upheaval, his mind ever striving, almost as in the Hamburg days, to take flight from its manifold intellectual themes to problems of a metaphysical nature—only now the urge and the agitation were more intense. I am tempted to compare this restlessness of the soul with the excitement preceding a journey, a condition which only occasionally yielded to a beautiful repose when, in our conversations, we would make plans for the future. We would talk of a house and garden on the Hohe Warte or in Grinzing,[1] or discuss the choice of a coffeehouse where we could meet of an afternoon. But, as a rule, such mental excursions ended in a gesture of the hand or a look of incredulity.

Unless I am mistaken, it was during the last summer that Mahler was to witness a strangely terrifying occurrence which depressed his thoughts. He told me that, while at work in his Composer's Cottage in Toblach, he was suddenly frightened by an indefinable noise. All at once, "something terribly dark" came rushing through the window and, when he jumped up in horror, he saw that he was in the presence of an eagle which filled the little room with its violence. The fearsome meeting was quickly over and the eagle disappeared as stormily as it had come. When Mahler sat down, exhausted by his fright, a crow came fluttering from under the sofa and flew out. The peaceful abode of musical absorption had become a battle-ground upon which one of the innumerable fights of "all against all" had taken place. Mahler's account of it still tingled

[1] Suburban districts of Vienna.

with the horror of so striking a demonstration of that cruelty of nature which had ever been one of the reasons for his deep world-sorrow.

In the autumn of 1910 he went to New York again, and, in February of 1911, news came of his severe illness. When, in April, he arrived in Paris to submit to a serum treatment I decided to visit him. There he lay, tortured victim of an insidious illness, his very soul affected by the struggle of the body, his mood gloomy and forbidding. A careful allusion to his work, made with the intention of leading his thoughts to a comforting subject, elicited only pessimistic utterances. I therefore avoided touching upon serious matters and confined my conversation to an endeavor to divert and entertain his mind with a variety of subjects. In this I succeeded, on the whole, and I even recall that my account of some remarks concerning art from the mouth of a well-known Philistine caused a chuckle in which traces of his one-time humor could be recognized. Upon one other occasion I was gladdened by a similar flash of good humor: feeling that he needed a shave, a young French barber was summoned in whom all the elegance of his profession and that of the nation seemed to be united. While he attended to his job with exaggerated finesse I saw in the eye of the patient something akin to amusement. Perhaps there rose to the surface of his memory the figure of some fantastic barber from a fairy-tale. When the young man had taken his leave with a graceful bow, Mahler gazed after him and murmured softly, but in a highly animated tone: "Farewell, oh scraper of beards!"

Often, however, my endeavors to amuse him were useless, and on his face there would be an expression of indifference. I am mindful of a sad reply he made when I tried to describe to him the future house and garden of which we had talked in Vienna in former days. He was silent for a while and then said: "That would be quite nice, but, as a matter of fact, I have now but one desire—to take enough digitalis to support my heart." Then, again, his deadly sadness would leave him for a while and he would listen with interest to what I had to tell him about Vienna and its musical happenings. In spite of an occasional manifestation of crossness at the mention of Vienna, the old attachment would come to the fore again and again and, when all is said, he liked nothing so much as to listen to tales of the familiar haunts. I had to leave after a few days and never exchanged another word with him. When I saw him again, he was dying.

He was brought to Vienna in May. The resentment, the residue of quite a number of disappointments during his days in Vienna, had not been able to stand up against the desire, in his serious condition, to go "home." Messages of friendship and reverence which found their way to his sick-bed gave him great pleasure. He died on the 18th of May. When, on the following evening, we transported the coffin to the chapel of the Grinzing cemetery a storm was raging and the rain came down in torrents, so that we could hardly make headway. The funeral took place in the presence of an immense crowd and in hushed silence. At the moment when the coffin was lowered, the sun burst through the clouds.

Re-Creative Work

At the Head of the Opera

Mahler's dramatic gifts were matched by those of the musician, and therein lay his importance as an operatic leader. At home on the stage as well as in music, he knew how to imbue with his fervor and spirit not only the scenic proceedings but also the musical execution, and to point to his artists the way to a consummation both of the dramatic and the musical demands of a work of art. He was a truly dramatic man: which is to say, a man of the highest vitality of heart and imagination. His soul would take a passionate interest in the despair of Alberich who had been robbed of the Ring, and in his heart would rage the wrath with which the dwarf hurled his curse at the robbers; he breathed anew with the prisoners of Pizarro as they were allowed to walk in the prison-yard for a few minutes; he stormed with the jealous husband whose suspicion seemed well founded that the lover of Mrs. Flood was hiding in the washing basket; with Wotan he was in a towering rage at the disloyalty of Brünhilde and, with Brünhilde, he tried to assuage the wrath of the father: no human emotion, and none that was divine, was alien to him—no petty spitefulness of Beckmesser too wicked, no St.-John's-Day mood of Hans Sachs too serene—he lived in everything and everything lived in him. And no matter how foreign a sentiment might be to his own nature, how contrary to his character, his imagination would enable him to place himself inside the most opposite person and in the strangest of situations. Thus, Mahler's heart was on the stage when he sat at the desk. He conducted or, rather, he produced the music in accordance with the drama.

A performance of *Lohengrin* under his direction which, as a young conductor and coming from Pressburg, I heard in Vienna, has set a lasting standard for me. In the quarrel scene between Ortrud and Elsa in front of the minister I suddenly realized the essential point to be observed in opera. Mahler not only conducted the orchestra to the singing of an alto, but his soul was with Ortrud, he was one with her, he carried singer and orchestra along with him into the turmoil of rebellion felt by the humiliated woman. Then, again, he was guided in his interpretation of the music by the fright of Elsa, by her indignation, and by her proud belief in Lohengrin. Thus he took into account not only the spirit of the music but—pre-eminently in this instance—the spirit of the drama. To be sure, in that scene from *Lohengrin* it was simple, for its music has, so to speak, no essential life of its own, Wagner himself having allotted to it an almost exclusively dramatic function. A more complicated task is offered by the so-called Mystery Ensemble. Here the music rises to a greater importance of its own, and yet, it is again the drama—*i.e.* Lohengrin's perplexity, Elsa's wavering, the various emotions of the other persons, and the general foreboding of impending disaster—which the music is meant to express. Higher demands are therefore to be met here: an interpretation out of the spirit of the music and, at the same time and to the same degree, out of the spirit of the drama.

No less profound was another impression which fruitfully complemented the *Lohengrin* experience: the second act of *Figaro* began and, at the sound of the first measure of the prelude to the aria of the Countess, one felt transported into the realm of absolute music. In its spirit sounded the song of the violins, the singing voice gave itself up to the pure delights of the music, the theater vanished, immersed in waves of music, and in its higher sphere the sorrows and the yearning of the Countess were dissolved. Not that one felt transported into a concert-hall, but as if one were well lost to the world, even to the world of the theater. Mahler had conjured up the spirit of the music which had now become the sovereign ruler. And how it engulfed the community of performers and listeners when Mahler called it forth in the floating ensemble movement of the reconciliation before the final presto of the fourth act!

Between the two poles which I have tried to indicate lives the art of the opera. Mahler's spirit ruled over its world from pole to pole. He felt precisely when the music should be allowed to develop all of its power and overflow the drama, and then, again, when and to what degree it should be subservient to the drama: in other words, when and in how far the dramatic proceedings should be permitted to predominate.

Just as he knew how to dramatize the music, he also endeavored—and therein lies the far more difficult problem of the opera—to fill the drama with the spirit of the music. He called upon the music to enlighten him and his singers as to the proper dramatic expression on the stage. More than that, since mimicry and gestures formed part of the dramatic expression, he saw to it that, in these directions, too, the suggestions and indications furnished by the music were obeyed. I am by no means alluding here to that co-ordination of music and gesture in the sense of the pantomime, as, for instance, the figures in the strings occurring at the time of Beckmesser's chalk scratchings or the music accompanying the silent play between Siegmund and Sieglinde and its exact execution. I am speaking here, above all, of the task of imbuing the atmosphere on the stage with the meaning of the music, to borrow from the music or to adapt to it the most subtle details of dramatic presentation—a glance, a smile—and not to permit a single gesture capable of interfering with the mood of the music. Mahler was able to penetrate to the very heart of the music, to visualize through the music the dramatic intentions of the composer, and he was aided by his extraordinary histrionic ability in practical demonstrations of how a scene should be played in order to make it blend with the music. He was thoroughly determined to abide by the directions of the composer. But only in the works of Wagner and in those of the post-Wagnerian literature do we find a "prestabilized harmony" between the music and the dramatic events. Mozart, although he, too, was a thorough dramatist in his music, had not yet given any dramatic directions over the observance of which Mahler might have watched. And yet, whoever has seen his *Figaro* will recall that finest and most inspired of comic performances at which every happening on the stage was in the closest relationship with the accompanying music.

As an example, let me cite the aria of Susanna: "Come closer, kneel at my feet," and the corresponding acting of the page, subtly suggested by the music. In the rehearsing of such a work Mahler followed no set method or principle, but merely his intuition and impulses. In his soul he carried the picture of the thoroughly familiar work, before him was the stage, and upon it the gifted artists: happy and inspired, his imagination sparkled up, drew enthusiasm from the dramatic situation and enlightenment from the music, was increased to still higher demands by the exceptional gifts of some individual artist or, if a performer should be found wanting, looked for easier means to achieve the desired expression. At the same time, this dramatic-musical practical application of his imagination was always entirely in the service of the work of art and never tempted him, in spite of its abundance, to be interesting on his own account. Mahler's aim was the unification and the musical penetration of music and drama.

His penetrating insight, however, could not fail to notice that an amalgamation of dramatic performance and music did not suffice to bring about the ideal of unity, and that, to accomplish it, it also needed the co-ordination of stage settings, costumes and lighting to the spirit of the action and music. At that important moment he met Alfred Roller who, from the point of view of the formative artist, had reached similar conclusions. In his sketches for *Tristan und Isolde* Mahler found the visual expression of a profound understanding of the work, and he now began to work jointly with Roller towards the realization of his idea of unity in operatic performances. While, up to that time, settings, costumes and light had sufficed to satisfy a generally cultured taste and to contribute interestingly to the general effect of a performance, their integral inclusion in the drama and their accommodation to its elements of style and its moods was still in its infancy, if it had ever been attempted at all. Roller, a painter with stereoscopic vision and alive to the needs of the theater, was, like Mahler, burning with a desire for the inspiriting of the scenic picture in opera. By using hugely proportioned, plastic stage settings he gave to the light an increased sphere of effectiveness and, in that manner, succeeded in placing the suggestive forces of lighting more effectively in the service of the drama and of music. Colors and forms grew out of the fundamental moods of the work and the costume was invested with its dramatic and spiritual function. The incomparable production of *Tristan* marked the beginning of the great epoch of Mahler's work in which he strove for the utmost of perfection. The complicated nature and novelty of his aims gave the impression, at times, of experimentation and caused public excitement and discussion; all the more so because, in the pursuit of new ways, mistakes and imperfections are unavoidable. Mahler's revival of *Don Giovanni*, which, of all the productions of that period, seemed to hold out the greatest promise for the future, also bore most strikingly the characteristic marks of the experiment and therefore became the object of especially heated comments. The excellent idea of making quick changes possible by the creation of a fixed stage frame suffered from the fact that the frame with its turrets could not unobtrusively and naturally blend with any of the scenic pictures. Again, there was a certain richness of color which formed a contrast with the quiet glow of Mozart's orchestra, and, finally, the choice of the singer for the principal part had not been a particularly happy one. The entire production, however, clearly showed up the problems Mahler and Roller were trying to solve, and, in retrospect, it appears to this day, and in spite of its deficiencies, as the most interesting and promising of that era. Every one of the following tasks profited by the preceding one until the apex was reached with Gluck's *Iphigenia in Aulis,* which my memory treasures as the most perfect interpretation of a stage work.

The way towards a unification of operatic performances and a consistent inspiriting of all their elements, a task to which he was the first to set his hand, was pursued by him to the very end. He knew how to make his co-workers out-do themselves in their artistic performances, which combined obedience to the demands of the work with personal achievement, and adaptation to the whole with a display of individuality. His own performance was remarkable for a most astonishing blending of painstaking devotion to the work—for only the work itself was of any consequence to him—and ingenious license. To be sure, the interpreter of dramatic art is permitted a considerably greater latitude than the conductor, for the theater still lacks a developed technique of annotations of stage proceedings equaling in exactness that of a musical score. Even the wealth of scenic directions in the Wagnerian drama, testifying, as it does, to a plastic vision of stage events, leaves more than one avenue open to license. All the more sensitive must be the conscience of the stage director who has to choose from the wealth of possibilities available to his imagination only that which is essential to the work, must avoid non-essentials and remain true to style in all of his instructions. Mahler's presentations were shining examples of this broad conception of loyalty to the work.

He felt impelled to make changes only if, because of vagueness, the original version was apt to render difficult the understanding of an important dramatic event, or if an easily remedied dramatic inadequacy should prove to be contrary to the composer's own intentions. Mozart and Wagner, of course, remained inviolable. In *Figaro* only did he venture to enlarge the court scene, thereby rendering more intelligible the meaning of Marzelline's suit against Figaro which, in the original, is somewhat vague. That, in so doing, he did not alter a single one of Mozart's notes is a matter of course. It was only a matter of transforming and enlarging a secco-recitative. A rather considerable interference with Goetz's *Taming of the Shrew* met with an interesting, though belated, justification. He had eliminated the weak final scenes of the opera which, in his version, ended with the beautiful duet of Catherine and Petrucchio. Although this version was highly successful he was pained by the very drastic operation, and said complainingly that one really ought not to deal in that way with someone else's work. How great was his relief when, in a piano score arranged by Goetz himself for a Mannheim performance, he found the same cut by the composer's own hand!

It goes without saying that, when he was not dealing with the greatest masters, like Mozart, Beethoven, Weber, Gluck, and Wagner, he felt a greater independence in his treatment of a work of art, but also a deep obligation to place at the composer's disposal his rich store of stage experience. It greatly benefited the performances of such operas as *Tales of Hoffmann*, *The White Lady*, *The Merry Wives of Windsor*, *The Jewess*, *The Taming of the Shrew*, and others, that his every interpretative license was employed solely in the interest of a perfect production, such as the composer must have visualized. He never had any doubts as to that vision once his intuition had penetrated into the very workshop of the composer. His profound familiarity with the latter's intentions always gave to his interpretations, in spite of all their daring, the impression of assurance and authenticity. Vain self-satisfaction because of a clever scenic idea was as foreign to him as the striving for purely theatrical effects. His labor only knew the laws emanating from the work itself, and this spirit of devotion governed his performances and, with them, the opera.

The Conductor

" . . . Past understanding are God's works and fair as at the birth of light"—thus, in *Faust,* the Archangel sings the praises of the creations of God, and the same enthusiasm for the masterpieces of music lived in the soul of Mahler. "Fair as at the birth of light" were they to him at every moment, did they sound in his playing, and did they appear to the listener, a prominent trait of his interpretation being this very impression of newness, improvisation, and spontaneity. Only the most profound understanding of a work reveals that remnant of incomprehensibility which is the property of the great creations of art and of nature and the mark of their greatness. It alone is able to kindle ever anew the flame of interest and enthusiasm, while the shallow-minded, thinking that they understand this composition to the very last or know that one thoroughly, soon lose their sense of proportion and become the victims of routine and triviality. His growing familiarity with the works of the masters but served to increase Mahler's amazement at and his admiration for that which was "past understanding" in them, and to give nourishment to his capacity for a constantly renewed relationship. Just as only constant wooing serves to keep love vigorous, so he, too, never ceased to woo the works of art and was ready at any time to revise his conception, or to improve and deepen it.

And that is the reason why none of his performances ever sounded hackneyed—every one of them, even the thirtieth repetition of the same work, took place "for the first time." It goes without saying that at the bottom of his apparently uncontrolled and impetuous production of music there was an inexorable exactness. He rendered strict obedience to the musical score, to the value of its notes, and to its directions concerning time, delivery, and dynamics, and demanded it of all his co-workers. He asked for an instrumental correctness from his singers and was never satisfied until the last measure of precision had been achieved by all. His insistence upon absolute musical clearness was commensurate with the clearness of his conducting and the exemplary beat of his baton, the distinctness of which was not impaired by even the most violent emotion. In the numerous performances under his guidance witnessed by me I may have noticed a mistake, now and then, on the part of a singer or a musician, but never a lack of precision or an inaccuracy in the ensemble, for the unfailing accuracy of his beat always knew how to keep stage and orchestra in perfect accord with each other.

At the same time, he never gave the impression of

machine-like precision, and I cannot recall that his exactitude was ever particularly mentioned either by his audiences or by the critics. The reason for this was that his precision was to him but a means to an end, and this end was—soulfulness. Without a sacred sense of order, leading almost to pedantry, the gifts of a genius were to him but an empty sound meaning nothing. When, however, he had succeeded, by his persistent demands upon singers and musicians, in achieving absolute distinctness and precision, the soul was permitted to spread its wings freely upon this secure foundation, and thus his performances produced the effect of spontaneous improvisation.

There was no arbitrariness at all in his interpretations. That he was accused of it merely proves the difference between his inspired presentation and that which was traditionally accepted. If he did make changes in classical works they were directed against the letter and in favor of the clearly recognized spirit. In that sense is to be explained, for instance, his much discussed retouching of the instrumentation of Beethoven's *Ninth* and other works. With his thorough knowledge of the orchestra, he interfered wherever the instrumentation was likely to mar the distinctness or the realization of Beethoven's intentions and, when he was attacked for it in Vienna, he defended his changes in a public declaration by pointing to the difference between the power of Beethoven's conception and the instrumental limitations of his day, the example set by Wagner, and to the duty to provide for a clear flow of the orchestral voices. The fanatical obedience to the score, which I have mentioned, did not blind him to any contradiction existing between its directions and the composer's actual intentions. I dare say that people are today generally convinced of the necessity of such retouching and the views diverge only as to the manner. At any rate, Mahler was actuated, in this respect, by the acuteness of his ear, which made him sense the musical meaning of vaguely instrumented passages.

"Your Beethoven is not my Beethoven," he replied resentfully to a well-meaning friend who had interrogated him on the unusual character of his performances. And that, indeed, explains the whole matter. His Beethoven had nothing in common with the polished classic habitually heard in routine-like concerts of the day. His relationship to him was born of experience, and fraught with experience was his interpretation. His *Fidelio* with the *Leonore Overture* and his indescribably fine rendition of the overture to *Coriolanus* have remained sufficiently clear in my memory to enable me to testify to the "Beethoven-nearness" of his nature. For in him were the thunderstorms of Beethoven's soul, its vigor, and its love; and in him, too, was simplicity and truth and the sense of the symphonic which, no matter how much care he bestowed upon details, always gave precedence to the organic form.

A look into the depths of the work, as piercing and full of divination as his, made arbitrariness and subjective conception impossible. Complete was the picture that stood before his inner vision and there was no gap to be filled on one's own authority. The frequent crime of arbitrary changes and subjective alterations of the meaning of works of art has its cause—where downright presumption or a craving for originality are not to blame—in the defective spiritual vision of an interpreting artist who has not been given the key to the heart of the work. What is there left for the poor fellow to do, if he wants to avoid a shallow performance, but to fill up the gaps arbitrarily on his own authority?

Mahler's clear vision of the works of the masters was not, however, the clearness of daylight. Music is by no means a daylight art and its backgrounds and its last depths are not disclosed to the man of the bright soul. From dark underground regions it springs and in dark underground moods is it understood and felt. Not the clear blue Mediterranean, but the darkly surging ocean, is kin to it. Dark, too, was the surging in Mahler's soul. Is it surprising, then, that it felt at home in the kindred element and was able to pierce the depths of music by virtue of its nocturnal vision?

"What is best in music is not to be found in the notes," Mahler was in the habit of saying. And this best and soulful element which surged with eloquent force from the music he performed produced so elemental an effect and one of so personal an avowal that doubts were entertained at times whether it was still the composer himself who spoke or whether Mahler's impetuous soul had not perhaps seized upon the musical language of the other man as a means of pouring out his own feelings. That Mahler desired nothing but to disclose to his very depths "the other man"—*i.e.* the work to be performed—is beyond any doubt. The question, however, whether, from such a production of music, the soul of the composer spoke, whether it was that of the interpreter, or a mixture of both, touches upon the real secret of musical re-creation. Only a positive avowal of one's ego, whether it be in life or in music, is able to carry conviction and to stir up deep emotions by the full force of its directness, and it is the failing of even the most sincerely meant mediocre interpretation that the identities of composer and interpreter are lacking, that an "I" tells us of a "he." How different is it in the case of an inspired interpreter! The expression of being "beside oneself" gains its most impressive meaning in the transports of his enthusiastic production of music. Ecstasy loosens within him the fetters of individualization and the re-creation of the other becomes a co-creation and almost a creation of his own. His gift resembles the ability of Proteus. Heart and imagination are so filled with "the other" that, in an excess of fellow-feeling, a kind of amalgamation takes place: the barriers separating the creating and the re-creating artist seem to disappear and the conductor now rules as over a work of his own. His it is to say "I," his to feel "I," and this very feeling of egoism gives to his interpretation its directness and its convincing power. It is for that reason that, in musical re-creation, serving loyalty and ruling license go hand in hand, and only he who understands that, under Wagner's baton, the *Ninth* sounded entirely in the spirit of Beethoven and that yet Wagner's own personality fully lived in it—nay, what is more, that only the unstinted pouring forth of Wagner's substance was able to set free the spirit of Beethoven—comprehends the essence of musical interpretation. And that is how it was with Mahler's conducting. By the full power of his great personality the work of the other man arose pure and strong and received its potent vital glow from the amalgamation of the two souls.

But even in cases where difficulties of understanding or the lack of an inner contact stand in the way

GUSTAV MAHLER CONDUCTING
As Depicted in Silhouettes by Dr. Otto Boehler

of a complete absorption of the other's individuality, subjective assurance and a realization of one's own individuality need by no means imply that violence is done to the composer. Mahler succeeded in presenting faithfully and, at the same time, with a full assertion of his own personality, even works which were somewhat foreign to his nature, much to the surprise of the composers themselves who were fully conscious of the gulf that separated them. Of decisive importance, if such endeavors are to be successful, is the "will to the other," in which Mahler, as an interpreter, was never lacking. In the presence of this serving loyalty—to allude to the teaching of that scholastic, mentioned by Jean Paul, according to whom forty thousand angels could dance on the point of a needle—all manifestations of the collaborating imagination may find room at every point in the firm structure of a genuine work of art without constricting the space taken up by the work itself, and it may even be said that without this wealth of sympathetic vibration of the mind and the soul its convincing realization cannot be achieved at all.

The visible picture of Mahler's conducting became very considerably simplified in the course of years. Boehler's excellent silhouette caricatures show the violent and drastic nature of his motions during his first years in Vienna. Although he was seated when conducting at the Opera, his agility at that time and also previously, in Hamburg, was astonishing. But it never produced the effect of exaggeration and superfluity, but rather that of fanatical adjuration. As time went on, his attitude and gestures became quieter. His technique of conducting had become so spiritualized that he was easily able to achieve a combination of unfettered playing and unfailing precision by his seemingly simple beat, his body remaining otherwise almost motionless. His powerful influence upon singers and musicians accomplished by a look and the most sparing of gestures what he had formerly endeavored to convey by violent motion. In his last years, his conducting presented a picture of almost uncanny quiet, although the intensity of expression did not suffer by it. I recall a performance of the *Sinfonia Domestica* by Strauss under Mahler's direction at which the contrast between the uproar of the orchestra and the immovable attitude of him who had unleashed it made a most eerie impression.

In spite of his absorption in the purely musical work with singers and musicians, on the occasion of stage rehearsals with orchestra the dramatist within him watched with the hundred eyes of Argus, and nothing on the stage, whether connected with the dramatic performance, with the lighting, or with the costumes, ever escaped him. Everything was under his observation at all times. By precept or teaching, at times in a quiet form and, then again, by violent attack, he accomplished the whole of his purpose with the performing artists. Not, however, because he set out to accomplish it, but because he must; and this powerful compulsion that governed him forced his co-workers through him to unquestioning obedience.

Let me once more refer to his warmness of heart as the most striking characteristic and strength of the conductor, a quality that imparted to his interpretations the impressiveness of a personal avowal and made one forget all the painstaking rehearsals, all traces of his educational work, all virtuosity and perfection of execution, and made the music he produced into a spontaneous message from soul to soul. In this borderland of artistic and human endeavor the nobility and strength of his soul proved true; the secret of the glory of the Opera's director and musical leader, which shines as bright today as ever, is explained by an ideal combination of artistic gifts and the emotional power of a great heart.

Creative Work

An elemental musical instinct lies at the bottom of Mahler's creative work. While the spiritual undertone of his music was at first a decidedly romantic one—I am thinking here of *Das klagende Lied* and the *Lieder eines fahrenden Gesellen*—his subsequent development shows the conflict and mixture of romantic and classic elements. To the classic attitude belongs his positive will to put the musical flow into solid forms, to curb and master his virile power, his imagination, and his emotions. Romantic—in a wider sense—is his daring and unbounded imagination, the "nocturnal" in him, the "nature sound," as is also his inclination to extremes, to excesses, and to the use even of the grotesque in order to achieve the desired expression, but, above all, the intermixing of poetic and other subjects of conception with his musical imagination. It was a violently agitated world of music, passionate humanity, poetic imagination, philosophic thought, and religious feelings with which he wrestled. Inasmuch, however, as, in addition to an exuberance of heart, he was gifted with both the inclination towards and the power of formulation, he succeeded in subjecting his highly individual musical language to the tyranny of symphonic forms, and this form became, in turn, the ruling idea of his creative work. He developed it to ever higher and new formations by the firm grasp of a substance which originally had bordered upon the chaotic in its diversity, richness, and fluctuation.

Even at the time when he wrote his *First Symphony* he was thoroughly under the spell of the symphonic idea, although, in its fundamental intentions, the work may be called the creed of his heart set to music. Beginning with the *Second,* he pursued more consciously and strictly the way of the symphonic artist who, from a thematic core, develops the construction of the movements with a close adherence to form and is enticed by no emotional excess, by no poetic idea, and even by no musical inspiration, to sacrifice the principle of the organic compactness of a movement. He continued, indeed, to develop the symphonic forms until their dimensions assumed gigantic proportions—especially in the realm of modulation with its intensified treatment of motives, as originated and developed by Beethoven—but his creations remained musical organisms, in which the thought of the whole was ever present in the formation of individual details. Here, then, we see him entirely in the footsteps of Beethoven. Moreover, there are Schubert and Bruckner influences in the melodiously joyful flow of some of the themes and in the occasionally gaily-Austrian character of the melodies. We are reminded of Bruckner also in the choral thematics of the *Second Symphony*, in the breadth of the symphonic conception and the inclination towards solemnity. Berlioz is recalled by Mahler's daring to bring the bizarre and grotesque within the scope of music in order to attain the ultimate in keenness of expression. No one, perhaps, had taught him so much about instrumentation as the ingenious Frenchman.

Another mark, too, is to be noticed at an important place in Mahler's genealogical tree: it stands for the "Unknown Musician" who symbolizes the masters of the folk-song, for an important part of Mahler's thematics, not only in his songs but also in his symphonies, has its origin in the folk-song—nay, it is folk-song. The poetic inspirations, too, which made his original musical springs flow, are derived from the intellectual and emotional sphere of folk-poetry. It was especially the lansquenet romanticism which touched a sympathetic chord in his heart and found expression in a considerable number of his songs. Mahler's youthful works, properly speaking, a *Nordic Symphony*, operas, and chamber music, are not known to me inasmuch as they were destroyed at an early date. I therefore do not know whether they, too, grew out of such "folk-like" sentiments or—and I am rather inclined to assume it —were inspired by the music of Schumann. At any rate, the youthful compositions, united in the first volume of the piano songs, show visible signs of Schumann's influence, with the exception of *Hans und Grethe*, a song charmingly reminiscent of the dance music of his German-Bohemian home.

The first work of larger proportions in which Mahler's essential nature appears in its full peculiarity has, at any rate, sprung from the soil of folk-poetry, even if it is not that of lansquenet romanticism. Grimm's fairy-tale of *The Singing Bone* was put into verse of his own and made the poetic foundation of *Das klagende Lied*, a composition for chorus, soloists, and orchestra. The music is inspired and thoroughly original and, at the same time, full of dramatic feeling and heart-felt humanity. The fairy-tale is followed by the more subjective romanticism of the *Lieder eines fahrenden Gesellen*, in whose poetry and music an impassioned experience has found artistic expression. Mahler's verses in both works seem to be fashioned, with a profound and sympathetic understanding, after the poetic accents of the verses in *The Youth's Magic Horn.*[1] Such, however, is not the case, for it is a fact that Mahler made the acquaintance of the Arnim-Brentano collection only a few years later. What a deep insight into his soul is gained, however, by the similarity of the tone of his verses and those of the poems which, at the time, were unknown to him! We recognize in it the affinity of his soul to that of the poets who presented us with the incomparable songs in *The Youth's Magic Horn.* His own, were they to be encountered among the latter, would differ from them as little as those by Arnim and Brentano themselves, who surely mixed their own poetic property with the poems collected by them. And, like the verses, their setting to music, too, has the character of a warm and imaginative popularity which reveals the roots of his artistic nature. When, later on, he made the acquaintance of *The Youth's Magic Horn,* he must have felt as if he had discovered his own native country.

In it he found everything that agitated his soul and he found it presented in the same manner in which he felt it: nature, piety, yearning, love, farewell, night, death, spectral doings, lansquenet man-

[1] *Des Knaben Wunderhorn,* a collection of German popular poems, by Arnim and Brentano.

ners, youthful spirits, nursery jokes, crisp humor—they all lived in him as well as in the poems. And so his songs flowed forth—through a happy union of original poetry with a music of profoundly similar character grew a number of the most charming works of art from which his personality, now virilely finished, stands forth in bold relief.

. . . . . .

Mahler's songs to texts from *The Youth's Magic Horn,* the earlier ones of which were with piano accompaniment and the later ones with orchestra, form a refreshing, varied, and characteristically essential part of his creative work. In every one of the songs we find tell-tale signs of productivity: an original musical idea. Not one of them is merely sentimental declamation. Without referring to them individually, I should like to call attention to the various realms of expression to which they belong, because they are rather instructive in connection with a clear understanding of Mahler's essential nature. Take the soldiers' songs: in addition to the high-spirited ones, like *Aus! Aus!* or *Trost im Unglück,* and the melancholy ones, like *Zu Strassburg auf der Schanz* and *Der Tambourgesell,* we find three songs in which the nocturnal element in Mahler's nature—there were entire provinces in the realm of his soul that never saw the light of the sun—speaks with the full force of that peculiar quality.

Der Schildwache Nachtlied is one of the most outstanding compositions from that comparatively early period. Night itself pulses in the words that pass between the boy and the girl, in the march of the nocturnal round, and in the ominous shudders of the ending. *Wo die schönen Trompeten blasen* is the most tender and heartfelt of the three, nocturnal, too, in its mood and moving in its ghostly ending. In the third, finally, the *Revelge,* we have a unique vision of the Mahler who felt himself kin to night and death. In the relentless marching, in the ghostlike coloring, and in the terrible intensity of feeling, we see a frightening manifestation of the demoniac nature of Mahler's soul.

Again, we find a number of devout songs: filled with a simple and profound faith is the music of the *Urlicht;* quite different that of the *Himmlische Leben,* a song in which devoutness appears in the garments of childlike imagination, and that of the similarly conceived *Es sungen drei Engel.* Greatly characteristic of Mahler are the humorous songs: *Selbstgefühl, Ablösung im Sommer* and *Des Antonius von Padua Fischpredigt.* The latter, from which Mahler took the thematic material for the ingenious scherzo of the *Second,* is a masterpiece of original invention, powerful humorous expression, and compactness of form. The droll *Ablösung im Sommer* furnished the main theme for the scherzo of the *Third.* Beautiful and heart-felt folk-songs are *Scheiden und Meiden* and *Nicht Wiedersehen;* above all, however, the fourth *Lied eines fahrenden Gesellen: Die zwei blauen Augen von meinem Schatz.* We find it again as the stirring central piece of the funeral march in the *First.*

One of the most important specimens of Mahler's earlier vocal compositions is *Das irdische Leben,* forming no part of any group of similar songs. It stands quite by itself and was highly thought of by him, as may be readily understood if it is considered that, in a naïve and vigorous manner, it expresses a deep world-sorrow, similar to that which Mahler himself felt throughout his life, except that his had the higher pathos of a passionately expansive nature. This song is also one of the first in which his full musical peculiarity manifests itself. No smile is so pleasing and infectious as that of a person with gloomy tendencies and, for that reason, the little group, "*Gesänge guter Laune*" are exceptionally charming. Among them are, for instance: *Verlorene Müh, Rheinlegendchen, Wer hat dies Liedlein erdacht.*

After finishing the *Fourth Symphony,* Mahler turned from popular poetry to its literary twin. He was attracted by Rückert's artistic mastery of the language, its profound veracity and simplicity being felt, in a certain sense, as a kindred trait. With the cycle of the *Kindertotenlieder*—in selecting the five most beautiful of the more-than-a-hundred poems he proved his exquisite poetic understanding—Mahler has created a soul-stirring specimen of lyric art. Just as the poems are in no sense popular poetry, so his music, too, is entirely removed from the popular mood of the former songs. Noble symphonic melodies form their musical substance, a fact which is true also of the five Rückert songs which followed. Among them, *Ich atmet einen linden Duft* is a jewel of melodic poetry, *Um Mitternacht* the uplifting evidence of his firm trust in God, and *Ich bin der Welt abhanden gekommen* deeply moving both as a song and as a most personal avowal of the soul. Common to all of these lyrics is their song-style. Even the most highly dramatic expression never led him to overstep the boundaries of the song-like.

The songs with orchestra accompaniment contain perhaps the most sublime achievements of his orchestral ability and are exemplary for the ideally shaded sound relations between singing voice and orchestra. The symphonic artist took a keen delight in indulging his formative faculty as a composer in the contracted form of the song. The master of instrumentation devoted especially loving care to his efforts to produce the most exquisite effects with the modest accompanying orchestra. Altogether, the diversity and wealth of contrasts in the songs of Mahler give us an impressive idea of the riches of his nature which, in his symphonies, reach imposing dimensions.

. . . . . .

Did this wealth of his nature correspond to an equal wealth in his music? Or, to put the question quite directly and bluntly: did Mahler have the gift of genuine musical invention? In speaking of his songs I have alluded to the original musical idea which was lacking in none of his songs. In the song, to be sure, everything depends upon the musical core itself, while, in the symphony, it is largely a question of what is being done with the idea. It may even be asserted, with slight exaggeration, that, in the song, the idea is the end, while, in the symphony, it is the means. However, the thematics of his symphonies, too, show the inspiration of the genuine, sound, and true maker of music who could never have developed great symphonic forms from a scanty little motive, to say nothing of an artificial thematic construction. He needed the continued stimulation of the inspired idea, of the theme which a blessed hour had produced, in order to be able to proceed with the inventive work in his symphonies. For, in a large sense, everything in music naturally depends upon invention: the substance as well as its symphonic application. Above all, however, the inventions of Mahler bear the imprint of his personality. Who is there to deny its originality? I consider it important to call attention to the fact that, in his thematics, I recognize both the classical and the romantic elements which correspond to the mixture in his nature. It should also be emphasized that, in the case of themes in the spirit of the folk-song and belonging to the latter category, we never have to do with imitations, let alone, adaptations. It is a genuine popular tone which rises from Mahler's music and which, as I have explained, corresponds to his nature.

The substance of the popular tone, however, has its counterpart in the theme, symphonic in the sense of Beethoven, broad in its construction, plastic in its motives, and in the germs of symphonic composition. As a matter of fact, even the principal theme of the final movement of the *First* is such a symphonic theme, only, in that case, the course of the movement is dependent upon the emotions rather than upon symphonic intentions. With the *Second*, one may even say, with the mighty initial measures of its very first theme the great symphonic artist enters upon his work and, at the same time, upon the succession to the classic symphony. The broad conception of the principal theme continues to be characteristic of Mahler and he even develops and enlarges its structure in his *Sixth* and *Seventh* and, above all, in his *Ninth*. As in the older symphonies, he usually places the male principal theme in opposition to the female singing theme. It is never of popular origin but—in the manner of the second themes in classical music—always belongs to the sphere of lyric art. A broadly spun solemn singing forms the thematic substance of the slow movement, a characteristic mark, also, of the works of Bruckner. The final movements, too, show the broad conception of symphonic thematics.

Special mention is due to the inspirations in his scherzi. As is but natural in a musician of so singular a sense of humor, the popular nature of the invention in his scherzi is on a correspondingly rare and unusual level. A special place in Mahler's creative work must be accorded to the scherzo of his *Second*, both as a whole and with regard to its musical inspiration. It undoubtedly represents a culminating point in the entire realm of symphonic scherzo literature. How droll and, at the same time, graceful is the inventive element in the scherzo of his *Third*, how mysteriously exciting and singular that of the second movement of his *Fourth!* The central idea of the scherzo of his *Fifth* is not humorous, but a striking expression of vital force. The trio of the scherzo of his *Sixth* is remarkable for an indication of the most singular charm of invention which is quite Mahler's own. The scherzo of his *Seventh* is a spook-like nocturnal piece, while, in the *Ninth*, with symphonic mastery and exquisite charm, he makes use of the Austrian slow country waltz.

On the whole, Mahler's music shows a leaning towards the use of the Austrian dialect. We hear it —reminiscent of Schubert—in the trio of the second movement of his *First* and—slightly resembling Haydn—in the main theme of the first movement of his *Fourth*. Sounds of Styria are heard in the above-mentioned slow waltz in the *Ninth*. The characteristic opening bar of Vienna's military bands, with its big drum and cymbals, found its way, in a witty quotation, into the march movement of his *Third*, while the military signal of retreat is to be heard in the scherzo of his *Third*. A reminder of the popular singers of Vienna is found in the secondary theme of the scherzo of the *Fourth*, and there is even a Vienna waltz in the scherzo of his *Fifth*. Quite in the Austrian manner, too, are the variations in the andante of the *Fourth*. Mahler's marches are full of the sound of Austrian military music, of which he was very fond. When he was two years old, a servant was in the habit of leaving him alone in a barrack-square so that she could be in the company of her soldier friend—and there, for the first time, he heard drums and trumpet signals and beheld marching soldiers. The romantic spirit of the military may frequently be observed in his creative work, possibly an after-effect of these childhood impressions of the barrack-square. The recall is sounded twice: the *Great Recall* in the final movement of his *Second*, symbolizing a call to the dead to assemble for the Last Judgment, and the very artistically formulated *Little Recall*, as Mahler himself called it, at the ending of the first movement of his *Fourth*. Of a military character, too, are the repeated trumpet signals in the introduction to the first movement of the *Third* and the wild music of the charge before its reprise which ends in a drummed march rhythm. Of a martially romantic character is the music of *Der Schildwache Nachtlied*, *Der Tambourgesell*, and *Revelge*.

The march plays an important part in the creative work of Mahler. In the *First* and in the *Fifth* there appears the funeral march, to which he gave the most singular tragi-ironic meaning, while a quickly energetic march dominates an important episode in the development of the finale of his *Second*. A substantial part of the first movement of the *Third* consists of a spirited march: *Der Sommer marschiert ein*. March rhythms are also to be found in the first movement of the *Sixth*, in the second movement of the *Seventh*, and in the finales of the *Fifth* and *Seventh*.

Mahler's thinking in the contrapuntal style begins with his *Second Symphony*. Its polyphonic construction and its tendency to form and transform motives point to the fact that the work originated in the time of Mahler's classical tendencies. His deep study of the problems of movement technique manifested itself increasingly until he had reached his *Ninth* and, beginning especially with the *Fifth,* led to a revolution in his style. For, far from being merely a poet who is proposing to set to music his poetic visions, Mahler was, as I said in the opening of this chapter, a genuine "producer" of music who, in plastic thematics, in the construction of a movement, in the development which includes every one of the motives, in the art of the counterpoint, and in the elaboration of the form of the sonata, the rondo, the fugue, etc., aimed at the accomplishment of a most exalted task of his own setting. The strong and simultaneous influence of thoughts, conceptions, and emotions in the first four of his symphonies gives way, from the *Fifth* to the *Seventh,* to a predominance of the purely musical picture. Between the two periods there are indications of a particular devotion to Bach, and it was especially the *Art of Fugue* which greatly influenced his contrapuntal work. There is evidence of this as well as of a concurrent tendency to elaborate the form of the rondo in the rondo-fugue of the *Fifth.* The exalted polyphony of the Veni creator spiritus in the *Eighth* and the contrapuntal mastery in the third movement of the *Ninth*, dedicated by him to the "Brothers in Apollo," show to what heights Mahler had developed the art of treating the orchestral voices. He also gave his special attention to the variation. He admired with all his heart the *Haydn Variations* of Brahms and was fond of explaining what a high conception of the idea of variation Brahms had shown in that composition. Only in the andante of the *Fourth* has Mahler written actual variations. After all, however, the transformation and elaboration of a motive, the "variant," which often is also the foundation of the variation, is likewise an important part of the ductus of the voices and had therefore always intensely occupied Mahler's mind. The art of varying assumed ever higher forms in his successive symphonies and also added to the beauty of his reprise and coda.

Mahler's art of instrumentation, the product of an incomparable faculty for vivid sound visualization and knowledge of the orchestra, also went through a period of important development. While he never permitted his magnificent sound imagination to lead him into attaching essential importance to color, he mainly used his special gift for orchestral sound effects for the sake of distinctness. Where a special color was needed for the portrayal of his intention, he mixed it from the most singular sound elements, as only his sublime coloristic talent was able to do. In view of the intensification of his polyphony, however, it took all of his skill of instrumentation to make clear the complicated tissue of the voices. In his *Fifth*, he even had considerable trouble in keeping pace with the complicated technique of the various movements.

It would be a worth-while task to devote a special essay to Mahler's art of instrumentation. Great importance would certainly attach to a theoretical discussion of the way pursued by him to bring about the intensification of the symphonic idea—*i.e.* the development of his polyphonic style, of his harmonics, of his technique of motive and variations, etc. In these pages, devoted as they are to general considerations, there is no place for professional investigations. They may, however, be recommended most warmly to young musicians interested in composition.

It is an opus of musical compactness that is presented to us in the creative work of Mahler, and the scrutinizing eye will find no gap in the musicological continuity and in the formal construction. Nevertheless, a purely musical valuation will never be able to do justice to his work, which is also the history of his inmost self. Only by looking upon his work as the musical manifestation of a great soul shall we have gained the correct point of view. Standards of humanity will have to be added to those of art if the creative work of Mahler is to be fully appreciated.

I shall endeavor to indicate the relationship of experience, thought, poetic vision, and religious feeling to his music by commenting individually upon his symphonies, his relationship to each one of them being a different one. Let me say this beforehand, however: He has never written "program music" —that is to say, the musical description of an extramusical event.

. . . . . .

I should like to call the *First Symphony* Mahler's *Werther*. In it he finds artistic relief from a heartrending experience. He does not illustrate in sound that which he had experienced—that would be "program music." But the mood of his soul, engendered by memory and present feeling, produces themes and influences the general direction of their development without, however, introducing itself forcibly into the musical issue. In that manner, a compact composition is born which, at the same time, is an avowal of the soul. It is not my intention to speak individually of the separate parts of the symphony.

The brilliant first movement, with its youthful fervor, and the vigorous scherzo, with the charming trio, need no explanatory words and, in fact, could not be benefited by them in view of their musical abundance.

The third movement, however, was, at the time, a new sound in music and its importance justifies a discussion. In the *Funeral March in the Manner of Callot* and the following finale the spiritual reaction to a tragic occurrence is transformed into music. In it the young composer relieves himself of his experience. In the vehemence of his emotions, Mahler was not conscious of his daring in expressing gloomily brooding despair and biting pain by this spectrally prowling canon, or by that music full of brazen derision and shrill laughter. The composition bears the imprint of ingenious inspiration, novelty, and unreserved veracity, and we need not be surprised at the fact that the first performance caused a great deal of perplexed wonderment. In the fourth movement, the raging vehemence of Mahler's nature breaks forth and, with relentless force, gains a triumphant victory over life.

Approximately in December 1909—that is, in the last year but one of his life—Mahler wrote me from America after a performance of the *First:* ". . . On the other hand, I was quite satisfied with this youthful sketch. How strangely I am affected by these works whenever I conduct them! A burning and painful sensation is crystallized. What a world this is that casts up such reflections of sounds and figures! Things like the Funeral March and the bursting of the storm which follows it seem to me a flaming indictment of the Creator. . . ."

This shows how the elemental power of expression of this music was able deeply to affect the composer himself after an interval of a number of years during which he had not heard it. The symphony has the typically unique power which the youthful work of a genius is able to exert by means of its superabundance of emotions, by the unconditional and unconscious courage to use new ways of expression, and by the wealth of invention. It is alive with musical ideas and with the pulse-beat of fervent passion.

In his subsequent works the composer turns away from personal experience. Following a primitive tendency of his soul, he looks upon the generally tragic fate of man and the vision is formed into the *nenia* in the first movement of the *Second*, a mourning-music born of world-sorrow. The movement begins and everybody feels: thus begins a symphony. The truly Beethovenesque greatness of the beginning takes hold of us with irresistible force. A tragic emotion held in check has been collected into a concentrated expression—the sinister theme opens the movement of a symphony, mighty in its invention, development, contrasts, and architecture—and the master has found his style. Formally, we have here a regular sonata movement consisting of first part, development, reprise, and coda. If we now turn from the loftily arched edifice with its brilliant lights and deep shadows, with its drastic contrasts and fateful conglomerations of the polyphonic musical language, to a consideration of the wholly inadequate term of "Funeral Service," the only one which Mahler himself was able to furnish when he was asked "what had been in his mind," who is there to venture, in view of the relation of this term to the music which it attempts to describe, to speak of "program music" as has actually been done?

It is true that, in the *First Symphony* and especially in its third and fourth movements, the music is thoroughly colored and influenced by occurrences in Mahler's life. The world of emotions and thoughts of the *Second* is, so to speak, more foreign to the music. In the first three movements it is nothing but a substratum of moods without any continuity in thought; neither has it, in an emotional sense, a steady influence upon the music which lives a life in accordance with its own laws. Moods, emotions, and thoughts are here dissolved within the music—they are changed into music. Still more absolutely musical than the first movement is the second, a charmingly agitated andante of a preponderantly gay character. In conversation, Mahler called it a friendly episode in the life of the hero whose funeral proceedings form the first movement. The third movement grew out of a sinister frame of mind—as if the chaos of life suddenly appeared unreal and ghost-like. It is not likely that this perhaps most original of Mahler's scherzi, full of fantastic life, with its sinister flow upon which play the flashes of a spirit of buffoonery, and with the nature-born lament which sounds from it, is based upon a definite conception or thought. It was born, rather, out of a mood of horror and grew into a masterpiece of symphonic music.

I should like to interrupt here the process of reflection to point out that not only may a composer's moods, ideas, and emotions be changed into music but that conversely, music also calls forth ideas. Nietzsche says in his *Birth of Tragedy from the Spirit of Music*, that music scatters about sparks of images and that it is quite within its essence to produce images which are quite different in character from those which, at the time of its birth, had sponsored it. A loose play between music and imagination frequently accompanies the process of creation; dream-like images are conjured up by the music and fade again, they stimulate it and lend to it sentiment and color, they interchange with thoughts and indefinite moods, while the music itself pursues its own way according to its own logic. Mahler himself testified to the disjointed dream-likeness of the spirit world which hovers over music when he related that, at the high-spirited finale of the first movement of his *First Symphony*, he had a vision of Beethoven who burst out laughing uproariously and then ran away. The laughing Beethoven had really nothing to do with the occurrence which, according to Mahler's own testimony, was the incentive for the composition of the *First Symphony*, and his intrusion is so "unprogammatic" that, more effectively than any aesthetic investigation, it shows up the absurdity of the assertion that Mahler's compositions are program music.

Similarly, Mahler said, in order to give an idea of the sinister mood of the scherzo of his *Second*, that it was as ghost-like as the far-away sight of dancing couples when no music was heard to accompany it —again a picture which makes impossible the assumption of a continuous thought guiding the composition of the symphony.

In its fourth movement, however—to return to my reflections—the sung word sounds forth and the rays of the Primordial Light pierce the opaque surging of the waves of sound which had their source in moods and had assumed their shape in accordance with their own laws. In the song, man sings—to use the devout words from *The Youth's Magic Horn*—of his trust that the dear Lord may vouchsafe him a little light to show the way into the blessed life beyond. Here, then, we have—almost—a program for the following movement: the wandering in the glow of the Primordial Light. Surely, that vision gave the general direction to the formation of the movement—the image here comes closer to the music. Mahler's imagination is filled with the "Last Judgment" and we are able to feel, at the beginning of the movement, how a sequence of mental pictures is in conflict with the musical sequence and triumphs over it, a process which is all the more readily understood when we consider the profound emotion of a man filled with his vision. Soon, however, with the march-like development of the choral themes, the symphonic musician grasps the reins more firmly, and it is not until the entrance of the *Great Recall* that poetic imagination is again allowed to take the lead. In his most noble setting to music of Klopstock's poem of the Resurrection, to which he added in verses of his own the expression of his hope and sure confidence, Mahler replies for the first time to the sorrows, the doubts, and the questions of his soul. In glorious sounds, to which the exalted annunciation has inspired him, and in a gradation kindled by the enthusiastic soaring of his yearning heart he attains, at the end, to the solemn security: "Die I shall, only to live," and "Arise, arise, my heart, thou shalt after brief rest, and thy beats will carry thee to God."

With a hopeful and heightened sense of living he

is now able to look about himself. "How beautiful the meadow seems today," says Parsifal as, with a feeling of solemnity, he looks upon nature. Such, too, is Mahler's emotion, and as, lovingly and deeply moved, he gazes upon nature he feels it, at the same time, within himself—its heart beats in his breast. The *Third Symphony*, in which often nature itself seems to have turned into sound, is the only one whose sequence of movements conforms to a series of imaginings. The original headings of the movements are: *Pan erwacht, Der Sommer marschiert ein, Was mir die Blumen auf der Wiese erzählen, Was mir die Tiere im Walde erzählen, Was mir die Nacht erzählt, Was mir die Morgenglocken erzählen, Was mir die Liebe erzählt.* Night speaks to him of man, the morning bells peel out tales of angels, and Love speaks to him of God—we see the simplicity of the mental understructure of the symphony. For the same reason, however, he was able again to leave out the titles, just as the scaffolding is removed once the house is completed. He wished that, undiverted, his work should now be interpreted in a purely musical way, and he was justified by the fact that it had become music.

One qualification, however, would seem to be in order: in the first movement, trumpet signals, beatings of drums, drastic vulgarities, fiery marches, majestic trombone solo, and humming trills of muted strings seem to indicate that a wealth of strange events and thoughts are to be described musically rather than that they have become music which, even by the titles of *Pan erwacht* and *Der Sommer marschiert ein*, would be quite insufficiently explained. And, as a matter of fact, there were quite a number of other strange subtitles, of which one, *Was mir das Felsgebirg erzählt*, has been mentioned by me before. Furthermore, he called *das Gesindel* that part of the composition which, with cellos and contrabasses, ushers in a grotesque episode. *Südsturm*, he called the wild passages of the strings towards the end of the composition. But even if all titles and subjects of imagination were cited, we would see to our astonishment that they by no means hang together and that quite a number of them are descriptive rather of images brought forth by the music than of music engendered by the image.

What, then, is it, as a matter of fact, that the movement really stands for? Two opposite fundamental Panic moods—eternal, rigid Being and wild, lust-impelled Growth—are transposed into a wealth of musical ideas. They are put into musical forms by Mahler and united in a symphonic movement of extraordinary architecture and, surely, also of extraordinary substance. New images and new thoughts are cast up by the moment in the ecstasies of creation. Disjointed as they are, they are apt to cause confusion rather than understanding and are by no means suitable for an embodiment in a program. I am ready to admit without reserve, however, that, in the case of this movement—and only in this—the wish to have it interpreted in a purely musical way may at times be obstructed by the intrusion of extra-musical elements—fantastic imaginings which impudently bob up in the course of the musical issue. And yet I feel that here, for once, a wild and untrammelled manifestation of genius should be permitted to outweigh problematics of style. When, in this movement, too, Mahler decided to do without any additional description, he trusted that the unique creation of an extravagant imagination would be accepted as a sound of nature, all the more so because, in the flickering glow of humor—which is the essential element of the movement—aesthetic boundary lines are apt to lose their distinctness.

Beginning with the second movement, things are different. If, while being absorbed in the nature of the flower, there came to his mind a tender and infinitely charming theme which he developed in a purely musical way, although still under the influence of the "flower mood," a piece of music would come into existence which could rightly claim to be Music but whose comprehension no longer depended upon the thought of the flower. On the other hand, in Berlioz's *Witches' Sabbath* from the *Symphonie Fantastique*, for instance, the idea of the phantom orgy must remain ever present in the mind so as to aid the understanding of the musical proceedings. And, like the second, the third movement, too, grew to be a specimen of Music. A world-dream had taken possession of his soul and it gushed forth in music, impelled by the loving agitation of the heart. However, when his dream, on its way past flowers and animals, had reached man, he longed for the word and, deeply moved by the human fate 'twixt joys and sorrows, he appended to the nocturnal music of the fourth movement Nietzsche's *Midnight Poem* which the thought of man had evoked within him.

Again, in the fifth movement, he needed the word to let the joyful message which lifted up his heart go forth from the mouth of angels. The hopeful thought expressed in a poem from *The Youth's Magic Horn* had at all times moved and elevated him:

> If you have sinned against God's law
> Go down on your knees in shame and awe—
> Pray to God both night and day
> And Heaven's joys will be yours alway!

From out of the angelic message grew the solemn

piece of music with the ringing bells, the joyful boys' and women's choruses, and the voice of sinful man who receives the blessed tidings. In the final movement, however, the word is hushed again—what language is there that could tell with greater force and stronger reason of Divine Love than that of pure music? The adagio, with its broad, solemn melodics, with occasional episodes of burning pain, but, on the whole, telling of solace and mercy, is one sound of fervently exalted emotion and, in a structural as well as in a musical sense, crowns the gigantic work. Mahler called the *Third* his *Gay Science* and, as a matter of fact, it is essentially an expression of the joys of life and of the world which his music communicates to us.

And, in the *Fourth*, it reaches even greater heights of a strangely exalted gaiety. "With wings that I have won I'll soar away," he had sung in his *Second*. He might have claimed the same, only in a more fantastic sense, for his soul's experience when he wrote his *Third*. For now he felt himself carried on high as in a dream and no longer was there any ground under his feet. An account of such a floating condition is given in the *Fourth*. In its final movement it even represents, thematically, a sequel to the "Angel Movement" of the *Third* and, in its general tone, follows its spiritual direction. After the works of pathos, a yearning for gaiety or, rather, for serenity had sprung up in Mahler's heart, and so he created the idyll of the *Fourth* in which a devout piety dreams its dream of Heaven. Dream-like and unreal, indeed, is the atmosphere of the work—a mysterious smile and a strange humor cover the solemnity which so clearly had been manifested in the *Third*. In the fairy-tale of the *Fourth* everything is floating and unburdened which, in his former works, had been mighty and pathetic—the mellow voice of an angel confirms what, in the *Second* and *Third*, a prophet had foreseen and pronounced in loud accents. The blissful feeling of exaltation and freedom from the world communicates itself to the character of the music—but, in contrast to the *Third*, from afar, as it were. The three orchestral movements take their course without a condensation of the peculiar moods out of which they grew into a definite idea. Not even the *Little Recall* in the first movement, mentioned before, is susceptible of a classification within a larger vision.

The first movement and the *Heavenly Life* are dominated by a droll humor which is in strange contrast to the beatific mood forming the key-note of the work. The scherzo is a sort of uncanny fairy-tale episode. Its demoniac violin solo and the graceful trio form an interesting counterpart to the other sections of the symphony without abandoning the character of lightness and mystery. Referring to the profound quiet and clear beauty of the andante, Mahler said to me that they were caused by his vision of one of the church sepulchers showing the recumbent stone image of the deceased with the arms crossed in eternal sleep. The poem whose setting to music forms the last movement depicts in words the atmosphere out of which the music of the *Fourth* grew. The childlike joys which it portrays are symbolic of heavenly bliss, and only when, at the very end, music is proclaimed the sublimest of joys is the humorous character gently changed into one of exalted solemnity.

In the first four symphonies an important part of the history of Mahler's soul is unfolded. The force of spiritual events is matched by the power of musical language. The correlation of the world of sound and that of imagination, thoughts, and emotions, is thus common to them both. While, however, in the *First* the subjective experience with its tempest of emotions is exerting its influence upon the music, metaphysical questions strive to find an answer and deliverance in music in the *Second* and in subsequent symphonies. Three times he gives the answer and every time from a new point of view. In the *Second* he asks the reason for the tragedy of human existence and is sure its justification is to be found in immortality. In the *Third*, with a feeling of reassurance, he looks out upon nature, runs the rounds of its circles, and finishes in the happy awareness that it is "almighty love that forms all things and preserves all things." In the *Fourth*, he assures himself and us of a sheltered security in the sublimely serene dream of a heavenly life.

He has had enough now of struggling with weapons of music for a philosophy of life. Feeling strong and equal to life, he is now aiming to write music as a musician. Thus the *Fifth Symphony* is born, a work of strength and sound self-reliance, its face turned squarely towards life, and its basic mood one of optimism. A mighty funeral march, followed by a violently agitated first movement, a scherzo of considerable dimensions, an adagietto, and a rondo-fugue, form the movements. Nothing in any of my conversations with Mahler and not a single note point to the influence of extra-musical thoughts or emotions upon the composition of the *Fifth*. It is music, passionate, wild, pathetic, buoyant, solemn, tender, full of all the sentiments of which the human heart is capable, but still "only" music, and no metaphysical questioning, not even from very far off, interferes with its purely musical course. On the other hand, the musician was all the more diligently striving to increase his symphonic ability and to create a new and higher type.

It was the *Fifth* whose intensified polyphony demanded a renewal of its style of instrumentation. Thus, with the instrumentation of the work, a new phase begins in the growth of Mahler, and in the *Fifth* the world has now a masterpiece which shows its creator at the summit of his life, of his power, and of his ability. In a certain sense, the *Sixth* and the *Seventh* belong to the *Fifth*. Both are also as metaphysical as music can be, and in both of them the composer aims at a further intensification of the symphonic idea. But the *Sixth* is the product of a decidedly pessimistic turn of mind, its fundamental mood being caused by the bitter taste in the potion of life. In contrast to the *Fifth*, it utters a decided "No," especially in its last movement, in which the relentlessness of the struggle of "all against all" seems to have been turned into music. "And therefore is existence burdensome, And death desirable, and life detested," could be its motto. Mahler called it his *Tragic Symphony*. The symphonic gradations and climaxes of the final movement resemble in their dismal power the towering waves of the ocean that rush at the ship and wreak destruction. The work ends in hopelessness and in darkness of the soul. In it he has uttered to the world his *non placet*. The work was uninfluenced by "that other world" which, from the very beginning, had not been within its field of vision.

The *Seventh* also belongs to the absolutely musical and purely orchestral group of symphonies. The word has been allotted no task of elucidating any of the imaginative contents of these three works and therefore they are lacking entirely in vocal passages. And, by the same token, I am deprived of the possibility of a detailed discussion, for I feel unable to speak about the music itself. Neither is there any reason why I should analyze it "professionally," because thorough analyses have been in existence for a long time. In the three central movements of the *Seventh*, however, highly important and humanly illuminating, that romanticism again makes its appearance which, it seemed, he had outgrown long ago. Emotional strains of an epoch lying in the far-away past come to the fore again in the three nocturnal pieces and reveal the fact that the master of the mighty first movement, of the radiant rondo, has to start all over again on the road of yearning and in quest of the answer the search for which is the task of his life.

At that significant moment of his life he happened upon the hymns of Hrabanus Maurus and he now collected all of his symphonic powers, intensified to the highest point, in order to reply to the yearning question of his heart with a musical creation of the utmost dimensions, his *Eighth Symphony*, with its Veni creator spiritus and Goethe's interpretation of immortality in the final scene of *Faust*. No other work of Mahler is so saturated with the spirit of fervent affirmation. It sounds from the wonders of the boisterous polyphony of the hymns which the master-hand of Mahler had formed into the temple structure of a compact symphonic movement. It sounds alike from the words of *Faust* and from the streams of music to which the feeling of deliverance had inspired Mahler. The seeker after God confirms in his advanced years and from a higher pedestal of life the assurance which, as a younger man and in the uplift of his heart, he had gained in the *Second.* The later creation shows an entire clearness of the relations between the world of thoughts and music. From the very beginning, the master had had recourse to the word, from the very beginning he had acknowledged that there were questions of eternity from which the symphony had grown and which in it should find their answer.

Can it really be the same man who, "in harmony with the infinite," had reared the structure of the *Eighth,* and whom we now meet again in the *Trinklied vom Jammer der Erde?* Who, in the autumn, lonely and languishing for comfort, softly steals to the beloved resting-place? Who, with the benevolent gaze of gentle old age, looks upon youth and, with kindly emotion, upon beauty? Who seeks to forget in intoxication the senselessness of mundane existence and, finally, takes his melancholy farewell? Is it the same master who, after the gigantic proportions of his symphonies, forms a new kind of unit consisting of six cantos?

It is hardly the same man, or the same composer. Up to that time, all his works had been born out of the emotions of life. In the knowledge, however, of the serious affection of his heart he had begun, like the wounded Prince Andrei in Tolstoi's *War and Peace*, to dissociate himself spiritually from the sphere of life—a loosening of all former connections had changed the entire aspect of his feelings—and *Das Lied von der Erde* was, as I have pointed out once before by alluding to one of Spinoza's expressions, a creation *sub specie mortis*. Earth is about to vanish from his sight, another air is wafted in, another light shines overhead, and thus it turns out to be an entirely new work of Mahler's: it has a new style of composition, a new kind of invention, of instrumentation, and of movement technique. It is a work more characteristic of his own self than any one ever written by him, not excluding even his *First*. That work had been marked by a consciousness of self, natural in a young and passionate man to whom his personal experience signifies the world. Now, however, while the world seems to vanish beneath him, the ego itself is turned into experiences, and a force of emotions which knows no limitations is seen to develop in him who is about to depart.

Every note he writes speaks only of himself, every word he sets to music, though it may have been written thousands of years ago, expresses but himself. *Das Lied von der Erde* is the most personal utterance in Mahler's creative work and perhaps in music. Invention, too, which, beginning with the *Sixth*, was occasionally of less importance in itself to the great symphonic artist than as mere material for his creative forming, regains its highly personal character and, in that sense, it is quite in order to call *Das Lied von der Erde* the most "Mahleresque" of his works.

The title of the last canto, *Der Abschied*—farewell—might have been used as a heading for the *Ninth*. Born of the same mood, but without musical connection with *Das Lied von der Erde*, and developed from his very own thematic material into a symphonic form which only he was able to create in his day, the first movement grew to be a tragically moving and noble paraphrase of the farewell feeling. A unique soaring between farewell sadness and a vision of the heavenly light—not a soaring of the imagination but one of his essential emotions—lifts the movement into an atmosphere of celestial bliss. Here, too, the invention is seen to be as personally Mahleresque as that of *Das Lied von der Erde*. The second movement, again in a new form of the intimately familiar scherzo and, in this instance, progressing in broad principal time, is remarkable for its great wealth of varying moods. A tragic undertone sounds in the joy and one feels that "the dance is over." In the defiantly agitated third movement Mahler once more furnishes most striking proof of his stupendous contrapuntal mastery. In the last movement he peacefully bids farewell to the world, the finale being like the melting of a cloud in the ethereal blue.

In its conception, technique of movement, and polyphony, the *Ninth* continues the line of the *Fifth*, *Sixth* and *Seventh*, but it is backed by a most intensive spiritual agitation: the feeling of leave-taking. And while it, too, is pure orchestral music, it differs from the central group and comes nearer again to the earlier symphonies by the strong influence of a so decidedly spiritual and fundamental mood.

. . . . . .

The new, daring, and revolutionary in our art must in the course of time unavoidably become well known, familiar, and customary. It is not the fact that a new land has been wrested from the sea which assures continuous life to the great thought of Faust or lasting value to the ground that has been gained. Mahler, adventurer of the soul, has also succeeded in wresting from the elements a new land in music which, after oft-repeated performances, will surely have lost its sensational character. It is even remarkable that, in our day, it still produces sensational effects. Emotion and the urge towards an unrestrained musical avowal had been too elemental to permit of an early familiarity with the symphonies. The daring spirit with which his music is alive still flames up high whenever it sounds forth. To be sure, even though Bach, Beethoven, and Wagner appear to us in the light of an assured possession, it is advisable to mistrust the interpretation, for Mahler, the conductor, has demonstrated the fact that it is possible to make these works sound again and again as if they were performed for the first time. Given an adequate performance, the titanic nature of the works is sure to be recognized even in our day.

The new in drama and music, on the other hand, enjoys the protective assistance of the congenial interpreter. But there is such a thing as a gradual fading away and, by and by, the sensation of daring is bound to pale and, especially in the event of inadequate interpretations, to become weaker and weaker. And this leads us to the question how far the daring and adventurous should be considered essential in a work of art. That which is purely daring, having its foundation pre-eminently in novelty and boldness, is destined to age quickly. Only a combination with deeper and more constant values may help it to attain lasting effectiveness. That the works of the masters of Promethean descent are stamped with the seal of immortality is due to their wealth of creative power, to their depth of emotion, and, above all, to their great beauty which in its essence is immortal and keeps the accompanying and more mortal charm of being "interesting" from fading.

And so the supreme value of Mahler's creative work does not lie in the newness which is so movingly revealed in the essential elements of an interesting, daring, adventurous, and bizarre character, but in the fact that this newness, with its added ingredients of beauty, inspiration, and soulfulness, has become music, and that the lasting values of artistic creative power and eminent humanity are at the bottom of his creations. This is why they have preserved their full vitality to this day, twenty-five years after his death, and will maintain it in the future.

Personality

THOSE WHO KNEW MAHLER WILL RECALL how often his facial expression would suddenly change from cheerfulness to gloom. It seemed as if he were reproaching himself for having thoughtlessly forgotten to remember something that was sad. The significance of these attacks of melancholy—in his later years they were perhaps less frequent but they never ceased altogether—became clear to me only gradually. At the bottom of his soul lay a profound world-sorrow whose rising cold waves would seize him in an icy grip.

"How dark is the foundation upon which our life rests," he once said to me with deep emotion, while his troubled look gave evidence of the convulsion of his soul from which he had just freed himself. And, haltingly, he continued, speaking of the problems of human existence: "Whence do we come? Whither does our road take us? Have I really willed this life, as Schopenhauer thinks, before I even was conceived? Why am I made to feel that I am free while yet I am constrained within my character as in a prison? What is the object of toil and sorrow? How am I to understand the cruelty and malice in the creations of a kind God? Will the meaning of life be finally revealed by death?"

In such and similar words laments, astonishment, and horror would pour from him as from a gushing spring. Fundamentally, there never was relief for him from the sorrowful struggle to fathom the meaning of human existence. Energetic activity would divert him, humor help him towards temporary release, while a deep interest in the spiritual life of humanity would strengthen him and assuage his unquenchable thirst for knowledge and instruction, but: "For what purpose?" remained the torturing basic question of his soul. From it grew the strongest spiritual impulses for his creative work, and every one of his creations must be considered another attempt to find the answer. And, no sooner had he found it, than the old question would again send forth from the depths of his heart the unappeasable call of yearning. For, such was his nature that, because of its inconstancy, he was unable to hold conquered spiritual positions. His life and activity were spent in impulses, and so he was forced again and again to renew his fight for spiritual possessions. It was for this reason that life, art, and personal relations seemed new to him from day to day, while the advantages of a systematic progress and of a complete mastery and use of a gain were denied to him. Every day he had to begin all over again, and every day he had to waste himself anew in struggle and surrender. He would have made but a poor hero for an educational novel, for steady development, methodical use (in the sense of Goethe) of that which he had experienced, thought, and acquired was not in his nature. The romanticist he was at heart was governed by the propitiousness or the unpropitiousness of the hour.

And yet it would be fundamentally wrong to think of him as vacillating and unstable. While he was not constant, the direction in which he pointed was firmly fixed and no impulse was able to swerve him from it. Neither ought he by any means to be called unhappy, for he who had been given so rich a substance, so warm a heart, and so eloquent a tongue, cannot be classified among either the happy or the unhappy. He knew of fervent exaltation and of bitter sorrow, and so strong an inward agitation is a finer gift of the gods than mere happiness. And as for sorrow, which, to be sure, was his faithful companion throughout life, Tasso's comfort was his, too:

And if, bereft of speech, man bears his pain,
A god gave me the gift to tell my sorrow.

His sorrow and his yearning became music, and just as they were reborn again and again, so they were turned ever anew into a work of art.

Ecstasies of yearning, of sorrow, and of exaltation, however, were not the only emotions upon which he knew how to express himself, for while he was inclined to be "beside himself," his spiritual gifts were yet sufficiently rich to enable him also to communicate himself inexhaustibly out of a more peaceful state of his soul. His spiritual climate was not exclusively rough and changeable. To be sure, there were frosts, heat, and storms within him, but mildness, too, and even warming blessed sunshine, a fact to which many a one of his compositions, as for instance the serene andante of the *Second* or the *Rheinlegendchen,* bears witness. He himself called the latter the beginning of a bit of sunshine. Smiles and gay outbursts of laughter suited his features as well as his character, but gloom, it must be admitted, was ever present on the threshold.

If, previously, I have called attention to the importance of the nocturnal element in his creative work, it is but meet that I now point out the corresponding side of his personality. In it is to be found the reason for the impression of a demoniac nature which so potently proceeded from him and which made him appear interesting to all and awe-inspiring to many. It will ever remain a secret of Nature how it could have created and made capable of living a man with such violent inner conflicts, and how it could have kneaded into a fundamentally sound and vital constitution so much of energy and intellectual acuteness, so much of serenity and self-sufficient quietness and, at the same time, so much of gloomy irritability, of danger from out of threatening depths, and, lastly, so much of whimsical humor. In view of his inability to enjoy the lasting possession of spiritual gains I feel unable to call him actually believing and devout, and this in spite of his religious inclinations and exaltations. He was able, in the uplift of his heart, to scale heights of belief, but a firm repose in faith was not vouchsafed to him. His heart was touched too deeply by the suffering of the creature. Murder among the animals, the evil that men do to each other, the sensitiveness of the body to disease, and the constant threats of fate—all this again and again shook the foundation of his faith, and it became the ever more conscious problem of his life how to reconcile world-sorrow and world-evil with divine kindness and omnipotence.

Just as he expressed questions and yearning in music, so it was music, in turn, that kept questions and yearning alive within him and kindled them ever anew, for music has an irresistible power to guide the soul in the direction of the Beyond. It not only scatters—in accordance with Nietzsche's words I have quoted—sparks of images but also seeds of faith. In its highest manifestation it is mysteriously kin to religion. Divine service needs music for the most solemn expression of devoutness, it lends convincing effect to the worshipful emotions engendered by the ecclesiastical texts or the religious proceedings in the Biblical oratorios and, beyond that and quite independently, as absolute music—as, for instance, in Mozart's or Beethoven's Andante—it causes exaltation and edification such as only religion itself could evoke.

It would be out of place to enter here upon a discussion of the close relationship between music and religion, but I should like to point out that the formative arts, too, frequently combine devoutness with music, and how natural and generally comprehensive an effect is produced by the music-making little figures which adorn the Bellinis' images of the Madonna and kindred works of art. Especially, however, does the "Concerto" by Giorgione come to mind in this connection. Here, indeed, they are not angels who play a music the floating lightness of which seems to be saturated with a spirit of Divinity, like the melodies of Mozart or Schubert. It is a pious monk who plays—not the elderly, quiet viola-da-gamba player of the painting, but a glowing, ascetic soul. We see a human eye that seems to be accustomed to search yearningly into heavenly distances. His are the fingers under whose touch strains of Beethoven could be made to sound. Of such a kind, too, seems to be Mahler's soul: from the earth whose affliction he suffers—seeking God. I repeat that Mahler's religious inclinations found nourishment again and again in this kinship of religion to music. Its transcendental power may not be able to affect musicians—and listeners—who, in spite of all their genuine musicality and saturation with music, are free from religious perceptions and presentiments. Those, however, whose souls are capable of soaring beyond terrestrial affairs will be confirmed and strengthened in their devoutness by music.

While his thoughts and yearnings carried him towards "The World Beyond," Goethe's words also have their application in this case: "This world's not silent to proficient man." Much as the Faustian man, as whom we have to regard him, felt impelled at all times to search for the ultimate meaning of all Being and Doing, he was, at the same time, attached by thousands of ties and interests to mundane Being and Doing, and also deeply interested in the spiritual life of humanity. He was, above all, powerfully attracted by the teachings of natural science and its progress. A physicist friend of his had to inform him frequently concerning the latest results of learned investigations down to the last scientific detail, and this friend could not say too much in praise of the acuteness of his understanding and the thoroughness of his searching questions.

In his reading he preferred to draw his learning concerning questions of natural science from the comprehensive and logical presentations of the philosophers. Lotze's *Microcosm* occupied him for quite a long time, and especially his atomic theory grew to be a most stimulating subject of thought. Fechner's *Zend-Avesta* made a lasting impression upon him, and the same author's *Nana, or the Soul-Life of the Plants,* was a source of real joy. That he was fascinated throughout his life by Goethe's general attitude towards nature, and by the great poet's wealth of writings on that subject, goes without saying.

Mahler should not, however, be considered, in this connection, as one who received without giving. His productive mind interested itself in the problems which, by means of books or oral communication, forced themselves on him. I recall the occasion when he undertook to interpret the law of the attractive power of the earth as one of the repellent effects of the sun, and that, when talking to his physicist friend, he endeavored in his impassioned manner to adduce other cosmic phenomena in support of his theory. When, in his presence, it was mentioned that, by cutting an earthworm in two, two specimens were produced, the hind part growing a new head and continuing to exist independently, he exclaimed immediately: "That would be proof against the entelechian teaching of Aristotle."

He was much too sensible and conscious of the deficiency of his practical equipment to be sure of the scientific significance of remarks of that kind. These and similar thoughts, however, interested him so deeply that he would not content himself simply with the absorption of knowledge. In his energy of thought, he could not help occupying himself intensely with these problems, and nothing would make him happier than the conviction that, by finding a sound basis for these theories, he had attained to a deeper understanding.

The splendid intuition which, in discussion, was manifested in his remarks never failed to elicit the admiration of his scientific friends. When I made his acquaintance in Hamburg he was quite under the influence of Schopenhauer. Nietzsche made a deep, although not a lasting, impression upon him. As for the latter's *Zarathustra,* one is inclined to say that Mahler felt attracted by the poetic fervor of the work and repelled by the essence of its thought. Nietzsche's anti-Wagnerianism aroused his indignation and, in later days, he turned away from him entirely. It is characteristic, too, that the master of great symphonic forms felt vexed with the maker of aphorisms. During the last years of his life, the philosophy of Hartmann seriously occupied his mind. The sun of his intellectual world, however, was Goethe, of whom he had an unusually comprehensive knowledge and whom he was fond of quoting, revealing an unlimited retentiveness of memory. Goethe's conversations, too, and not only those with Eckermann, were frequently the subject of his reading; and the conversation with Falk concerning immortality was one of the fixed points of his intellectual existence.

Of the German poets, Hölderlin was especially dear to him. Poems like *Patmos* or *The Rhine* were always in his mind and belonged to his sacred literary possessions. Deeply moved, he would quote to me from the magnificently obscure verses which Hölderlin had written after having been seized with his mental illness. Of the mystics, he was perhaps fondest of Angelus Silesius. He had the feeling of a veritable kinship with him and liked to find solace in his daring and exalted nearness to God. Mahler's fondness for Jean Paul is proved by the very fact that he named his first symphony after *Titan*. We often talked about the great novel and the figure of Roquairol, especially, whose influence may be sensed in the funeral march of the *First*. Mahler asserted that, more or less, every gifted man carried within himself such a Roquairol—that is to say, a self-reflecting, decomposing, scoffing, and imperiling spirit—and that he could gain the full mastery of his real productive powers only after having overcome it. He felt very much at home in the wildly complicated humor of Schoppe. His favorite work was *Der Siebenkäs,* which he pronounced to be Jean Paul's most perfect creation. It is natural that, especially in his younger years, his heart went out to E. Th. A. Hoffmann whose mind was so congenial to his. The poet's glowing imagination, his buoyancy, his humor, and, not least of all, the nocturnal side of his nature, strongly attracted him.

For reasons of humor, Sterne's *Tristram Shandy* also was among his favorite books. Mahler often said that without humor, the antidote for the poisons of life, he would have been unable to bear up under the tragedy of human existence. He was fond of referring in his conversations to matters such as the habits and maxims of old Shandy, to the opening of the will in Jean Paul's *Years of Indiscretion,* to details in Dostoievsky's *A Silly Affair,* and to similar literary incidents, and these allusions never failed to elicit his loud and hearty laughter. His own sense of humor often took the shape of droll fancies and he was also the possessor of a keen wit. He appreciated other people's aptitude for repartee and was fond of the most harmless of fun. His attitude towards the telling of jokes, however, was one of decided disapproval. He would, on such occasions, not move a muscle of his face, and even would be out of sorts for a while, as if it had been distressing to him. Coarse words were quite unbearable to him, and I do not recall that they were ever used in his presence or that he himself ever used one. But blunt utterances that had their justification in the style of the time, like those found in the works of Shakespeare, Cervantes, Sterne, and others, were as welcome to him as everything else that belonged to the nature of art. A passionate spiritual relationship connected him with the works of Dostoievsky, who had greatly influenced his general view of the world. In the conversation between Ivan and Aliosha from the *Brothers Karamazov* we find a fundamental expression of all that I have called Mahler's world-sorrow.

I have, of course, been able to cite but a few examples to prove Mahler's infinitely varied and comprehensive contact with intellectual matters. He found his way to the formative arts at a comparatively late date, and there never was any vital relation with them for the artist of the ear, of sound, of passion, and of the nocturnal. Rembrandt, whose nature was undoubtedly congenial to him, affected him perhaps most strongly of all. He never felt the art of the eye as a vital necessity, while, on the other hand, poetry and literature, and even natural science and philosophy, were indispensable to him.

The multiplicity of his interests should not be taken for the amateurish inclination of an unstable mind. The criterion of an amateurish culture is an accumulation of knowledge without assimilation. Mahler absorbed with unfailing judgment only such intellectual food as was apt to strengthen him for his life's task. He felt impelled to seek a deeper meaning in all occurrences, in life, and in suffering, and his striving for knowledge was the purposeful acquisition of a mental armor for that undertaking. In his explorations of the spiritual world the needle of his compass pointed steadily in one direction—upward. And so he did not only read or receive the substance of learning, but he passed through it, assimilating what instruction he gathered, and subordinating to this tendency towards metaphysical perception all of his striving for knowledge. Thus, his many-sidedness was, as a matter of fact, but a seeming one, and one would be able to speak with greater justification of the magnificent one-sidedness of a musician in whom the same flame burned for both his musical creation and his intellectual striving, lighting and pointing the way to the one goal. At the same time, it should be realized that in Mahler's acquisition of knowledge it was by no means a consciously systematic thought which guided and determined his educational process. Here, too, he followed only his impulses, and the truly magnificent process of acquiring intellectual values was unable to create within him a complete view of the world in which his restless heart could find comfort and repose. He remained true to his style of living: there was a constancy of direction, but a sequence of impulses rather than a carefully planned continuity.

The many-sidedness of Mahler's intellectual interests was most aptly mirrored in his conversation. The same man who was lovingly filled with the cosmic idea of creation, who was sorrowfully brooding over the sufferings of the world, who searched for instruction through all the intellectual realms to which he had access, who endeavored to find in music, by ever-increasing accomplishments, release from his inward struggles—that same man was also revealed in his conversation. The wealth and variety of his intellectual powers, the warmth of his emotions, and the firmness of his judgment, were matched by the thematic inexhaustibility, vitality, and assurance of his speech. Mahler was fond of conversation, and had not the frequent fault of being inattentive when others were speaking. He was able not only to speak but also to listen. He had the virtue of spending himself freely in conversation.

I recall many a conversation which had its beginning in the coffee-house in the afternoon, was continued throughout a long walk and ran through our common evening meal with undiminished vivacity. It was his habit, on such occasions, to assure me on parting that we had now definitely solved the seven riddles of the universe and that therefore everything was perfectly all right.

The improvising faculty and inclination which formed so essential an element of his re-creating activity also lent the inexhaustible charm of surprise to his conversation. When, out for a walk along the banks of a mountain stream, a musician lamented the fact that the possibilities of music seemed to be exhausted and that nothing could possibly come after Beethoven, Wagner, Bruckner, and others, he stood still and, pointing to the stream, called out in a tone of surprise: "Why, look there, my friend!" "What is it?" the other asked in surprise. "The last wave!" was the reply.

I was told of that conversation by others, but I personally recall a very characteristic reply from his lips when, in speaking of a new composition, I said that it was interesting. He replied: "Interesting is easy, beautiful difficult."

His presence of mind and his faculty for trenchant expression frequently led him to make remarks which were more startling than convincing. But though he occasionally succumbed to the temptations offered by his gift he was quickly and with the utmost seriousness again engrossed in practical discussion. The real charm of his conversation was that, independent of its substance, it never became anything else; in other words, in spite of all of its depth and importance it always retained the elements of ease, informality, and pleasant zest. At no time was Mahler more amiable than in his conversation which, though the substance was of the lightest, never deteriorated into chat or, when the subject was weighty, became a lecture.

As a moral individual, Mahler was frequently misjudged, and there were instances when admiration for the artist was accompanied by disapproval of his character. The warmth of his heart, his affection for his friends, and his deep interest in others, speak so beautifully and plainly out of his collected letters that, in order to refute the wrong judgments, I need but to recommend that they should be read by those in search of a true picture of his character. The cause of the misunderstanding may be that, while he had infinite powers of compassion, of rejoicing with others, and of readiness to help, it was but natural that, with the absent-minded look of the creative genius, he, most of the time, took no notice of his fellow-man and passed him by. Ethics molded into forms of methodical application cannot possibly be developed in a man whose enormous spiritual substance compels creative concentration. When another's want would pierce his consciousness he was ready to help and make sacrifices. He, who was full of the faculty for love, as is proved by his music, loved humanity but, in common with, we might say, all productive minds, he often forgot man. When he did perceive him he became accessible to his needs; but usually his gaze was directed inward.

I was in the habit of calling his relationship to friends one of "intermittent loyalty," for he was apt to spend considerable periods in total physical and spiritual separation from them. But, once the isolation was ended he was quite himself again, displaying all his warmth and sympathy. He was quite free from paltriness. Money meant nothing to him, and when, at the age of forty-seven, he left Vienna and thoughts of the future began to force themselves upon him, it was really the first time that he had any desire to make money. How little Mahler was subject to the professional afflictions of vanity and a mania for success is shown by his thankless concert programs. When he was invited to give a number of concerts in Petersburg, I told him of my misgivings due to the lack of attractiveness of his proposed programs. He was quite taken aback and exclaimed: "Why, I never thought of that!"

And when, following my exceptions, he had arranged other programs, he showed me one of them and asked: "Well, is this sufficiently productive of applause?" The droll expression was eloquent of Mahler's disdain of applause and success. Vanity was foreign to a mind directed solely towards the object itself, and outspoken praise even unbearable. But he had the faculty of accurately estimating his own importance and strength, and no amount of opposition and hostility was able to shake it. While steadfast in the face of belittlement of his own accomplishments and ungrudging of the well-earned success of others, he knew well the painful feeling of indignation when the unworthy triumphed. Schiller's words, "I saw the sacred wreaths of glory defiled on many a vulgar brow," were often quoted by him in connection with the all-too-frequent worship of false gods.

Referring to his outward conduct towards people, let me admit once more that, from the standpoint of social conventions, it left much to be desired. He, whose heart was full of kindness, could be hard and cutting, violent and hot-tempered, cold and forbidding. He was, however, always sincere. Despite his dominating professional position, this son of nature was never able to acquire polish nor the customary careless pleasantness of manner, neither had he any ambitions in that direction. His was a commanding personality which unconsciously demanded that others should adapt themselves to him; and they usually did.

The foregoing and, as it were, vertical contemplation of his spiritual and mental nature needs to be complemented by the aspect of the horizontal—that is to say, the daily course of the innumerable impressions out of which my present fixed image of his personality has gradually been shaped. During the seventeen years of our contact, in the flux of his growth and the changing light of events, it had, of course, appeared to me only in flowing contours. Attempting, then, to direct my contemplation to the development of Mahler's nature during that time, I believe I am justified—with the reservations which every attempt at classifying a living process requires —to divide it into three epochs whose temporal boundaries seem to me almost to coincide with those of his creative work, his re-creative activity, and his personality. First epoch: the seeking, suffering, impetuous and youthfully vigorous man, closely affiliated in his creative work with the nature-bound popular world of emotions of *The Youth's Magic Horn*—that is to say, up to the time of the completion of the *Fourth Symphony* (1900), and including, in his re-creative activity, the first years of an exuberant display of strength as the director of the Vienna Opera. Second epoch: the man at the summit of his strength and power, his gaze, in a certain sense, more definitely directed towards the "here" and "today," the re-creative artist waging with steadfastness of aim the fight with the surrounding forces for the attainment of his artistic goals and being influenced, in his creative work, by the poetry of Rückert, including his *Fifth*, *Sixth*, *Seventh*, and *Eighth Symphonies* (1907). Third epoch: loosening of his grip on the surrounding world, turning away from the will-to-do, directing his gaze again into far distances; as a conductor—with the exception of his performances of the *Seventh* and *Eighth*—removed from my observation through his activity in the United States; deeply impressed, as a creative artist, by Chinese lyric art and finding his consummation in *Das Lied von der Erde* and his *Ninth Symphony*.

His main theme, as I should like to call the yearning after God of him who suffered so much from the world, the constant of his life, dominated the first epoch and was accompanied by a great closeness to nature. It was akin to Faust's relation to nature when he said to the Deity: " 'Twas not the stranger's short permitted privilege of momentary wonder that Thou gavest; no, Thou hast given me into her deep breast as into a friend's secret heart to look; . . . thus teaching me to recognize and love my brothers in still grove, or air, or stream." But

Mahler's relationship went even beyond that, it was more "elemental." In a letter which he addressed to the publisher of a musical periodical, in 1896, he wrote: "I think it strange that most people, in speaking of 'nature,' always think only of flowers, little birds, the aroma of the forest, etc. The god Dionysius, the great Pan, nobody knows." How well he himself knew him is shown in the first, the Panic, movement of his *Third Symphony*. In spite of his Dionysian saturation with nature, however, and in spite of all creature-like devotion to it, he was by no means a Pantheist, a fact which is proved by the last movement. *Was mir die Liebe erzählt* had been his original title for it, to which he had joined the verse: "O Father, look upon my pain, And let no creature plead in vain." Neither these words nor, above all, the Adagio itself speak of a deification of nature, but they are eloquent of a heart-felt personal religiousness.

I consider it the great moral accomplishment of his life that he never acquiesced in the pain of the creature and in the spiritual suffering of mankind with the shoulder-shrugging *ignorabimus* of the philosopher, so that he might be able undisturbed to direct his gaze towards the beautiful and beatific in the world. "Not Father only of this world, but Czar!"—these words from the funeral celebration of Mickiewicz he, too, was able to say to God in his gloomy moments. But, then again, he felt that somewhere there must be a misunderstanding, and so he remained true to the task which had chosen him: to suffer and to seek in it a divine purpose.

During the second epoch, the son of nature, the God-seeker, experienced, although in a very limited sense, a sort of adaptation to that world which unavoidably is the atmosphere for the exercise of art. The work of art, born of the solitude of the creative artist, needs for its realization the great institutions usually to be found in a metropolis and their audiences. Ten years of unbounded devotion to such an institution and of the accompanying human intercourse and influences could not pass without rubbing off some of the roughness and singularity of the eccentric. There was enough of oddity and queerness left in him to make people wonder anew every day. To a friendly admonition he once replied: "The wild oats man has to sow are as a rule the best part of him," and when a well-meaning high official once advised him not to butt his head against the wall, he said: "Why not? There'll be a hole in the wall!" And yet, it is proved by the fact that his incumbency at the Vienna Opera lasted ten years that, although not assimilated, he had at least become acclimatized. And how did the God-seeker fare in this second and "temporal" epoch? He who wrestled with the world and had to wring achievements from it, was forced to direct his gaze towards it. The higher life dwelt within him and always determined his direction, but it was hidden beneath the effect he had upon the world. And while it was the source from which sprang the *Fifth*, *Sixth*, and *Seventh Symphonies*, it did not manifest itself dominatingly in their course.

Towards the end of this epoch, the metaphysical urge in this Faustian man once more burst all its dams in an excess of strength. The *Eighth* is born, the "Dispenser of Joy," as he called it. He sings the hymn to the creator spiritus, his question and his yearning are uttered with increased force, they find release and peace in Goethe's pronouncement in the final scene of *Faust*, and with this recurrence of his life's theme in its most sublime expression ends the period of deeds and begins the third epoch.

Now again his gaze is averted from the world. The heart, however, is failing and he has forebodings of death. It was then that the God-seeker experienced his severest crisis, and he refers to it in a letter to me in July 1908: "If I am again to find the way back to my own self I shall have to deliver myself up to the terrors of solitude. But, after all, I speak in riddles anyway, for what took place within me and still takes place, you do not know. By no means, however, is it that hypochondriac fear of death, as you surmise. That I must die is no news to me. But, without attempting here to describe to you or to explain that for which there are perhaps no words at all, I merely want to say to you that, at one fell stroke, I have lost everything of clearness and assurance that I had ever won for myself; and that now, at the end of my life, I must learn anew how to walk and stand."

And how does he overcome the crisis? The Chinese poems are in his hands, he sings *Das Lied von der Erde!* And just as once, when barely nineteen, he closed a letter to a friend with the words: "Oh, my beloved Earth, when, ah when will you take the forsaken one to your bosom . . . oh, receive him who is lonely and restless, All-Eternal Mother!", so now he who was doomed to death ends the work which was his very own with the words: "The Beloved Earth is clad anew in robes of Spring . . . and from afar eternal shine the Heavens, eternal, eternal. . . ." The loving greeting to the Earth lived in the heart of the young as well as in that of the aging man. Now, dominated by the feeling of farewell, it fills his entire soul. The *Ninth*, too, which came later, is expressive of it.

And so he overcame his last crisis, though in the sense of that place in the monologue of Faust where, thinking of deliverance through the poison-cup, he says: "Outspread, like ocean, Life and Day Shine with a glow of welcoming: Calm at my feet the glorious mirror lies, And tempts to far-off shores with smiles from other skies!" The gaze upon the dear Earth was but a backward look. The world stretches before the departing traveler in the mild glow of beauty, and this spiritual condition—in the very shadow of death and gazing upon life—furnishes the key to the following passage in a letter written in the early part of the year 1909: "There is so very much to write about myself that I cannot even make an attempt to begin. My life is now so infinitely full of experiences (since a year and a half ago),"—that is to say, since he had become aware of the affection of his heart—"I can hardly talk about it. How should I attempt to describe so appalling a crisis! I see everything in a new light—feel so much alive. I should not be surprised at times if suddenly I should notice that I had a new body (like Faust in the last scene). I am thirsting for life more than ever and find the 'habit of existence' sweeter than ever. These days of my life are really like the Sibylline books. . . . How foolish it is to suffer oneself to be submerged by the brutal vortex of life; to be untrue even for a short hour to one's self and to the higher things above us. But I am only writing this quite thoughtlessly—for at the next opportunity, let us say, when I leave this room, I shall certainly be quite as foolish as all others. What is it, after all, that thinks within us? And what acts within us?" And now follows the splendid and deeply illuminating sentence: "Strange! When I hear music—even while I conduct—I can hear quite definite answers to all of my questions and feel entirely clear and sure. Or rather, I feel quite clearly that they are no questions at all."

The new light in which he saw everything came from that very world. True comfort for his world-sorrow, he finally recognized—after all his thinking, yearning, and striving—came from music itself, which, as I have tried to express once before, is a way to God akin to religion. On many previous occasions, when Mahler was asked what he believed, he had answered: "I am a musician, that tells everything!" That he was apt to "weaken," as he hinted in a passage of the letter just quoted, only shows that even the most exalted of men have to pay tribute to the general instability of human nature, and all the more so if, like Mahler, they are so strongly governed by impulses. It was infinitely sad, however, that towards the end his acute illness feverishly beclouded his exalted spiritual condition. Up to that time, the transcendental aloofness expressed in *Das Lied von der Erde* and in his *Ninth* had held sway within him. And that he kept on asking questions and wanted, ever again, to "learn" reminds one of Tolstoi's beautiful legend of the three devout old men whom the bishop visited on their island. They made him teach them the Lord's Prayer over and over again because they were unable to retain it. When he finally had succeeded and his ship had long since left the island, they came to him one night, running over the waves, because, once more, they had forgotten it. But he said, deeply moved: "Why, you are walking on the waves—what further need is there for you to learn?"

And so it was with Mahler: he possessed and knew so much more than he asked, for in him was Music, in him was Love. And I think that, at the last, he will have found out that in the very fact of his faithful seeking lay the answer—and his long yearnings will be appeased.

GUSTAV MAHLER

BY ERNST KŘENEK

Bronze Head of Gustav Mahler by Auguste Rodin

Bohemian, Jew, German, Austrian

Many peculiar traits in Gustav Mahler's life and work become clear and understandable once one realizes that he was Austrian. The full implication of this simple fact hardly occurs to the minds of most commentators on Mahler because the notion of what "Austrianity" means is almost forgotten in a generation that cherishes the illusion of clear-cut national discriminations. In the light of such simplifying views Mahler was either a German, or a Bohemian, or a Jew. But classification in neither of these categories can explain his personality, nor do justice to the characteristics of his work.

Gustav Mahler was a Bohemian Jew, according to purely statistical data. He was born on July 7, 1860, the second child of Bernhard and Marie Mahler. Ten more brothers and sisters were to follow him, most of them doomed to pass away in their early youth. The town of his birth was Kališt, in Southern Bohemia, a purely Czech settlement. The nearby township of Iglau (Jihlava in Czech language), situated at the Western edge of Moravia, however, is largely inhabited by Germans, a "linguistic island." This condition was typical in many parts of Czechoslovakia and accounted for the interminable racial trouble ever freshly nourished by the increasing nationalistic tendencies of the 19th century. The Jewish minority, scattered all over the country, was at that time almost invariably counted into the German element. Most of the country Jews were merchants trading between the German centers in the towns and the solid mass of Czech farmers and peasants that surrounded those "islands." They spoke Czech with their rural customers but their social ambitions associated them with the German element because of its closer relations to Vienna, the center of the Empire.

Shortly after Gustav's birth the family moved into Iglau. Here he grew up in predominantly German surroundings. His first musical instructors, however, the *Kapellmeister* of the civic theater and a piano teacher, had distinctly Czech names. Gustav Mahler attended the grammar school and in 1869, two years earlier than was usual, he entered the Gymnasium, the public high school with emphasis on the classical languages. It would seem that it was his outstanding musical proficiency which caused his parents to send him to Vienna in 1875, a move which probably implied some sort of sacrifice on their part. In Vienna, he concentrated on his musical studies at the Conservatory of the Society of Friends of Music, then a private institution, which later became the Imperial Academy of Music. He finished his high school education simultaneously, so that he was able to enter the University of Vienna in 1877 where for two years he took courses in philosophy, history of art, and music.

Nothing is left of Mahler's compositions of this period but the titles. Ruthless self-criticism moved the young composer to destroy these works soon after he had written them. It is not without significance that one of the early works of the young Bohemian Jew was a *Nordic Symphony*. He does not seem to have been bothered by racial considerations at all. The titles of two operas—*The Argonauts* and *Ernest, Duke of Swabia*—give further evidence of the fact that Mahler's imagination was apparently caught by the pretentious display of mythical materials typical of the late romantic style which was swinging into full power with the first Bayreuth festivals. At all times a young composer of eminent gifts will instinctively turn to the most progressive idiom available. In the seventies, and for some decades thereafter, Richard Wagner's achievements, labeled "Zukunftsmusik" (music of the future), irresistibly attracted forward-looking young composers everywhere.

The Vienna Conservatory seems to have been a not too reactionary place at that time, since Gustav Mahler, in spite of his Wagnerian leanings, was a distinctly successful student. Some of his chamber music compositions were awarded prizes by the faculty. While the Conservatory courses provided the indispensable technical knowledge, his musical studies at the University brought him in contact with Anton Bruckner, an acquaintance which probably was of great influence in the formation of Mahler's personality.

Mahler and Bruckner

PUBLIC OPINION HAS A CURIOUS PROPENSITY for putting together heroes of the past in pairs whenever circumstances suggest such grouping. Bach and Handel, Goethe and Schiller are such legendary inseparables, no matter how unlike and even uncongenial they may have been in life. Bruckner and Mahler are frequently so linked, and it is true that they have certain superficial traits in common: both were Austrian composers of the later 19th century, and both wrote nine rather lengthy symphonies.

However, beyond these facts there is little resemblance. Anton Bruckner was, to begin with, Mahler's senior by more than thirty years. He was of German Catholic peasant stock, a native of Upper Austria, and remained throughout life a shy and somewhat self-conscious country schoolteacher, respectfully and yet hopelessly entangled in the goings-on of the big world. A man of extremely slow development, he never dared to believe in his own maturity and accomplishments and was an easy prey both to well- and ill-disposed friends, who manipulated his scores at will according to their opportunistic designs. His unshakable faith in God and Richard Wagner enabled him to carry out his unwieldy artistic plans despite opposition, intrigue and ridicule. His refuge was the organ which he played gloriously and it is under the great organ of St. Florian Abbey in Upper Austria that he lies awaiting the ultimate call of his eternal Master.

When Mahler came to Vienna, Bruckner was instructor in counterpoint at the University, a position which did not amount to much since musical theory at European universities was usually offered only as auxiliary information for musicologists. It would be interesting to know with what feelings the elder musician, wrestling with ever unconquerable symphonic difficulties, looked upon the nervous, talkative Jewish boy from Bohemia. It is, by the way, a telling sign of the innermost identity of creative genius, regardless of the personality of its possessor, that they developed a lasting friendship despite the difference in age and mentality. The mutual attraction between Jewish intellectuality and endemic naïveté is also a peculiarly Austrian phenomenon.

It is quite characteristic that Bruckner, in spite of the venerable simplicity of his mind, generally avoided the obvious and seemingly commonplace features which made, and still make, Mahler's music shocking to many of his critics. Bruckner's work is expressive of his conviction that the late romantic idiom was susceptible of unlimited evolution on its own terms; at any rate he did not worry about what should become of it. The disconcerting musical straightforwardness of Mahler, denounced by his adversaries as blatant and vulgar, is a striking foretoken of the great intellectual crisis which with extraordinary sensitivity he felt looming in the oncoming 20th century. His regression to primitive musical substances is more obvious and more far-reaching than Bruckner's analogous trend. Both were quite clearly oriented toward Franz Schubert, but while one would always recognize Bruckner's style as an organic development of the Schubert idiom, one is frequently struck by some of Mahler's tunes which seem as if they were actually quoted from Schubert, though brought into a new, strange context. I will later again refer to this important factor of "quotation" in Mahler's music. It is precisely what gives his reversion to previous styles more progressive significance than the more concealed and apparently more refined retrospectiveness of Bruckner.

Both composers have in common the truly symphonic spirit, the propensity for the monumental simplicity of the fundamental themes, the sense of the magnitude of gesture. In Bruckner all that is an outgrowth of his unshaken faith in lasting progress; in Mahler it is arrived at through an ever-present exertion of will power, under the strain of the impending crisis of the symphonic form and the tonal idiom. To Bruckner, the Catholic of age-old tradition, his faith was unproblematical, like the air he breathed. To Mahler, who later underwent religious conversion, relation to the Supreme Being was a matter of endless concern and ever-renewed discussion. The actual sphere of common interest for Bruckner and Mahler was undoubtedly their admiration for Wagner. Bruckner had enough confidence in his young friend to entrust him with the preparation of the piano arrangement of his Third Symphony which he had dedicated to the master of Bayreuth. Mahler acknowledged the significance of his intercourse with the elder composer in a beautiful statement answering the moot question as to whether he should be considered Bruckner's disciple. He also manifested his esteem for Bruckner actively as soon as he could, by including Bruckner's compositions in the programs of his concerts. This, however, did not happen until 1886, and he had a hard and long road to travel until he could apply himself to such worthy tasks.

Odyssey Through the Operatic Province

Like nearly every student, Mahler was faced with bitter disillusionment when, after graduating from the Conservatory, he had to leave the lofty realm of study for the laborious drudgery of everyday life. He had to accept humble jobs, such as giving piano lessons to the son of a rich Hungarian country squire and conducting miserable operettas at the shabby summer theater of Bad Hall, a modest spa in Upper Austria. His letters from this period reveal the exaggerated emotionalism of a sensitive youth plunged for the first time into the struggle of life. His manner of writing betrays his reading preferences: the rampant, tortuous and often ornate prose of the German romanticists, E. Th. A. Hoffmann, Jean Paul, and others. Some of his most passionate outbursts of grief over the hostile and terrifying world even read like quotations from some of these romantic authors.

This is the emotional atmosphere of *Das Klagende Lied*, the earliest of Mahler's compositions to have been preserved and one which he completed during those years of hardship. Perhaps more original than his earlier, lost musical utterances, it is probably because of this originality that it was turned down by the judges for the Beethoven Prize to whom Mahler submitted his "cantata." The jury was headed by the determined anti-Wagnerites, Brahms and Hanslick.

Somewhat more rewarding work was assigned to Mahler in 1881 and 1882 when he became conductor at the small opera houses in Laibach (later called Ljubljana, in Western Yugoslavia) and Olmütz (Olomouc, in Moravia). However, this modest advancement served only to increase his ambition, and he left Olmütz hardly less unhappy than he had embarked on his stage career at Bad Hall.

Although the intellectual circles with which Mahler came in touch at these places were mostly part of the Germanic top layer spread all over the Austrian monarchy, we may assume that his activities in various parts of the polyglot Empire enhanced his sense of universality, which is so characteristic of Mahler's music as well as of all truly symphonic music since Beethoven. It is certainly more than a mere coincidence that this symphonic style was first developed in Vienna and remained at home there as long as the Empire lasted.

From Olmütz Mahler for the first time went abroad, to fill the position of assistant conductor at the Royal Prussian Court Theater of Kassel in central Germany. On the way he stopped in Bayreuth and watched the first performance of *Parsifal* after Wagner's death which had occurred in February of that year, 1883. The pomp and circumstance of the occasion did not fail to produce the impression one might have expected on the young Wagner addict and confirmed him in his aspirations.

Measuring Kassel against Bayreuth rather than against Laibach and Olmütz, Mahler could not help being disappointed once more, although the resources of the Royal Theater were doubtless superior to those that had so far been available to him. When he confided his disappointment in a moving letter to the famous Hans von Bülow, who had conducted a concert in Kassel, the great man did his young colleague an unkind turn by handing over the letter to Mahler's superiors in the theater administration. Bülow's conscience, however, seems to have troubled him, for only two years later, when he was called upon to recommend candidates for an opening at the Berlin Opera House, he mentioned Mahler.

Mahler's operatic deeds in Kassel did not make history to any noticeable extent. However, his conducting at the summer music festival of Hannoversch-Münden (a picturesque little town not far from Kassel) left such an impression on his bewildered contemporaries that recollection of the event had not completely vanished when this writer came to Kassel in 1925 in a function similar to that of Mahler's forty years before. In a frenzy of energy, dashing back and forth through the backwoods of Hessia, the young fanatic had welded together several heterogeneous rural glee clubs to form an imposing vocal body for the oratorio performances. No matter how much these rustics may have hated Mahler for the ordeal of endless rehearsals, they were taken aback by the miraculous results which he obtained and prepared him a magnificent ovation at the festival.

Prague and Leipzig

His success was not apt, of course, to improve his position at the theater whose administration had been infuriated against him ever since Bülow's tactless behavior. Thus Mahler was glad to receive an appointment for one year at the German Opera House in Prague. Almost at the same time he received a call from the opera house of Leipzig which he accepted for the ensuing year because he had misgivings as to the measure of independence he would enjoy in Prague. The situation there soon took a very satisfactory turn, however, when Mahler's superior, the Wagner disciple Seidl, unexpectedly left for America. But the general conditions at the Prague Opera House were still not ideal. Catering to a linguistic minority, the institution had but limited financial resources. The director, Angelo Neumann, had the reputation of being a theatrical genius; at the same time he had certain speculative traits of the traveling company impresario of earlier times, probably not too propitious for serious, systematic artistic work. However, Mahler so appreciated his independence, even under such limitations, that he regretted having signed up for Leipzig where he should again have to deal with a superior, this time the eminent Arthur Nikisch.

His efforts to cancel the engagement were of no avail and served only to impair his position at Leipzig from the outset. He could not get along with Nikisch, and the atmosphere was soon embittered by the usual quarrels as to who should conduct what operas, about promises supposedly given and allegedly broken.

A highlight of Mahler's activities in Leipzig was the successful revival of Carl Maria von Weber's opera *Die drei Pintos* which Mahler had completed from the sketches Weber had left and from additional material of his own making. Weber's grandson who lived in Leipzig had persuaded Mahler to undertake this delicate task. The city of Leipzig being, for some reason or other, particularly Weber-conscious, the venture was received with much public appreciation. Some of the critics, however, in spite of the excellent opportunity of getting first hand information from Weber's grandson who owned the original sketches, as well as from Mahler who had elaborated on these sketches, held numerous passages of the original which Mahler had left untouched to be additions of the arranger alien to Weber's style, and praised others that were purely of Mahler's making as particularly fine specimens of Weber's inventiveness.

Professional Dilemma
Creator and Interpreter

IT WAS MAHLER'S LAST SEMI-CREATIVE CONtribution to the operatic art. At the time of his Leipzig engagement he was already working at full blast on his *First Symphony*, some of the thematic material of which he selected from a song cycle—*Lieder eines fahrenden Gesellen*—composed earlier in Kassel. His embarking on such a vast creative project soon made his situation in Leipzig altogether untenable. He certainly did not actually neglect his duties at the theater, but he limited himself to rendering the absolutely necessary services which apparently did not satisfy his superiors. The director chose the contemptible method of making life miserable for Mahler by appointing someone whose sole function was to disturb rehearsals and undermine Mahler's authority with the singers, and thus forced his resignation by trying his patience beyond the breaking point.

This was the first, and only evident conflict between Mahler the composer and Mahler the conductor. Many admirers of Mahler's genius regret that he had to waste his time and energy in dealing with the artistic insufficiencies of his fellow workers and concern his creative mind with the mean business of backstage intrigue. It is, of course, easy to condemn most of Mahler's employers and subordinates in his theatrical career for their lack of understanding of his significance as a composer. However, proficiency in the theatrical sphere is a product of explosive vitality rather than of contemplative intelligence. All energetic resources are focussed on the one moment when the given material is to be "put across" in a sort of spasmodic exertion of the whole personality. The creative process, however, is one of protracted, persistent penetration of the subject matter. And yet, the creator profits not only because of the valuable control over the tools which is gained by such contacts, but, above all, because genius feeds on the experiencing of the very distance between the abstract ideal and the contingencies of the material world in which his creations are destined to live. The interpreters of the work of art, on the other hand, need the co-operation of the creator because he alone can bestow lasting significance upon the performance by raising it to the level of the higher plan underlying the work. Mahler was amazingly at home in both spheres; hence the intensity of his conflicts with the single-track minds of average interpreters.

Operas

Why Did Mahler Not Write Any?

It is quite obvious that Mahler immensely enjoyed his theatrical work no matter how often he claimed to loath it. He needed those constant clashes with reality for the very creative work which they seemed to curtail to a dangerous extent. He needed ever renewed proof of the limitations of this world in order to retain the feeling of terrific tension which is so characteristic of his music. On the other hand, the tireless effort of striving for perfect performances is also understandable as a reaction to the challenging inertia of matter, as a persistent endeavor to find out to what extent matter can be vanquished by the spirit. Surely Mahler could have found other means to earn his livelihood: as a teacher, pianist, or in some other musical profession. However, any one of these activities would have involved the same frictions and tensions because of the high standards he would everywhere have exacted. Thus it is no wonder that he stuck to the theatrical career in spite of the interminable disappointments it generated, because the musical stage was his particular vocation.

At the height of his career, during those glorious ten years in Vienna, he was not only responsible for the musical aspects of his task, the direction of the orchestra and the supervision of the singers; he was the animator of the whole, conductor, stage director and designer, though assisted in the non-musical departments by eminent experts.

How is it that an artist of so comprehensive a theatrical talent did not endeavor to create works for the magic medium of the musical stage? There is an obvious difference between a dramatic and a theatrical composer. This can be clearly seen in comparing, for instance, Mozart and Beethoven. Mozart was an eminent theatrical composer. An inexhaustible wealth of amazingly differentiated nuances of expression assisted him when he animated his dramatic characters with musical life. His non-theatrical music, however, sounds relatively detached and self-sustained, as compared with Beethoven's symphonic utterances which are filled to the brim with the dramatic element of striking antitheses. Thus are Mahler's symphonies. The main difference between a dramatic and a theatrical composer seems to consist in the intensity and nature of the extra-musical associations that stimulate their imagination. While the dramatic feeling of the former is completely absorbed in the musical substance, the latter needs the impersonation of dramatic conflicts in theatrical characters in order to actualize the dramatic side of his musical inventiveness. Nonetheless, the dramatic composer may have an extraordinary feeling for the stage, as was the case with Gustav Mahler.

Budapest

Mahler is for the First Time His Own Master

WHEN MAHLER FOUND HIMSELF OUSTED from the Leipzig Opera House in the summer of 1888, his situation was rather critical. His health had suffered so that he had to undergo intensive medical treatment. At the same time he had to worry about the declining health of his aging parents. And no new post was yet in sight. However, his reputation was well enough established by this time and he had not to wait long for an interesting proposition to turn up.

The Royal Opera House in Budapest, founded but a few years before, was in very unsatisfactory condition because of poor management. The Commissioner in charge of the theatrical enterprises of the Crown cast his eye upon Mahler, who had become known as a tireless, efficient worker. A contract was drawn up which testified to the fairness as well as to the realistic pessimism of the court official. Mahler's services were secured for ten years at a generous salary. The new director of the opera house was given to understand, however, that a premature termination of this arrangement was to be expected if and when a certain political constellation should change, in which case Mahler would be payed off properly. This is precisely what happened after little more than two years, although Mahler had succeeded in making over a second rate, deficit-ridden provincial stage into a highly prosperous and artistically impeccable opera house whose achievements were praised far beyond the limits of the Hungarian-speaking area.

Apart from the predicted trouble caused by the political change, Mahler had made a nuisance of himself by the very measures which had brought about the splendid success of his management. For the first time he was not only a conductor responsible for the musical department, but the director of the whole, endowed with power to carry out his ideas as thoroughly as he could wish. One of his key ideas was the complete integration of drama and music, the dream of all truly theatrical composers since Monteverdi. Richard Wagner, the first to think the problem through with utmost consequence, had made it the business of his life to build up a training center where the integral musico-dramatic style as he conceived it would be taught and demonstrated in its purest incarnation. In order to insure this effect against any interference, he made Bayreuth into a hallowed shrine of the German nation so that the magic spell would not only hold adversaries in awe but also engender the necessary furor in the disciples who were to act as missionaries of the new artistic gospel all over the world. With his unerring comprehension of the mental structure of the period, Wagner had done exactly the right thing. The fact that his musico-dramatic style became in relatively short time a dominating feature in the development of music, and gained considerable influence on thinking even beyond the field of music, was due to the numbers of perfectly trained interpreters and propagandists who gradually occupied key positions in many important places.

Mahler's ideas on the performing of operas were a further development of Wagner's doctrine. Opera should be more than a display of costly voices and pretty tunes, more than a highly refined entertainment for the *élite;* it should be a manifestation of artistic thought, an integration of music, words, action and scenery of the utmost significance and complexity. All these diverse elements should be co-ordinated, each remaining in its own way a perfectly articulate symbol of the idea which had generated the miraculous art of opera.

In order to reach this objective Mahler did away with the traditional "star" system. Singers who thought their main business on the stage was to produce beautiful tones, in order to draw applause from listeners enjoying purely sensuous reactions, were of no use to him. He replaced them by gifted young artists whom he could mold according to his more comprehensive ideas. Their young and sometimes undeveloped voices were frequently a cause of disappointment to those inveterate opera-goers who did not care much for the sense and meaning of the spectacle and merely wanted to sit back and indulge themselves in the display of appealing sound.

Another feature of the Budapest experiment equally in line with Mahler's general principles was that he insisted on having all operas sung in Hungarian. In view of the fact that the question of whether opera in America should be given in English still arouses considerable discussion, it is no wonder that Mahler's innovation was frowned upon as a most revolutionary venture fifty years ago. And yet, it is obvious that if opera is looked upon as an integration of music and drama, the drama must be understood by the audience. Of course, there are many who pretend that they enjoy opera best when they shut their eyes and dream along with the stream of music, paying no attention whatever to the progress of the dramatic vehicle. This attitude requires a talent for abstraction which is an attribute of highly sophisticated minds; on the other hand, it is a sort of escapism in that a listener indulging in this practice capitulates before the complexity of the phenomenon which he is invited to take in and picks out just that single aspect of it which appeals immediately to his senses. The "man-in-the-street," however, wants to know what is going on if he is confronted with actors moving on a stage, and he is right. If opera is expected to become an intrinsic part of the artistic life of a nation it has to be intelligible in all its features. As long as it encourages the selection of some of them for special enjoyment it will not get anywhere beyond the state of catering to the taste of a small, and nowadays dwindling, minority.

The spectacular increase of audiences in the Budapest Opera House during Mahler's management proved his point entirely. His insistence on the vernacular far from made his task easier since he did not speak Hungarian and had to communicate with many of the artists through interpreters. Anyone who knows what it means to coach inexperienced singers in unusual assignments will readily understand that this was a backbreaking undertaking. However, Mahler had at least the satisfaction that many of the artists were filled with genuine enthusiasm for his ideas, methods and personality.

Hamburg
The Youth's Magic Horn

THIS CIRCUMSTANCE, THE GENEROUS SETTLE-ment, and the fact that he was forewarned of the impending crisis may have fortified Mahler when he again had to change the scene of his activities in the spring of 1891. In Hamburg, where he was called from Budapest, he was again merely *Kapellmeister* instead of general manager of the opera house. But working conditions seem to have been quite satisfactory on the whole since Mahler was to keep this position for the ensuing six years without serious trouble. He still frequently complained about overwork and exhaustion, about resistance on the part of lazy and unwilling musicians. But he could not help going about his job with an indomitable will to final perfection, which inevitably meant pouring out his energy to the last ounce and challenging the opposition of the omnipresent mediocrities.

Mahler had the great satisfaction of having his outstanding competence as a conductor formally acknowledged by Hans von Bülow, who at that time was director of the Hamburg Symphony Orchestra and whom he succeeded in this post after Bülow's death. Shortly before, Brahms, too, had testified enthusiastically to Mahler's superior qualities as an interpreter, after having heard one of Mahler's last Mozart performances in Budapest.

It is rather strange that both of these eminent musicians fully recognized Mahler's genius as far as his conducting was concerned and yet remained completely averse to him as a composer. At first one might assume that their judgment was based on the current (and usually justified) distrust of *Kapellmeister Musik*—music manufactured by conductors relying on experience rather than originality. Both Brahms and Bülow doubtless were connoisseurs enough to discover that Mahler could by no means be disposed of under this category. Even Mahler's early compositions are obviously original, although the idiom, the musical stuff of which they are made up, does not seem to us so alarmingly different from that of Brahms. Particularly the song cycle, which furnished some of the principal themes and the general atmosphere for

Mahler's first symphony, actually reminds one of certain Brahmsian lyricisms. And yet, Mahler was in Brahms's opinion "the most incorrigible revolutionist." Were men like Brahms and Bülow obstructed from perceiving those analogies by some novel features in the treatment of the traditional idiom, by unusual details of orchestration and the like, or did they divine the new, disquieting spirit looming beneath the relatively familiar surface? It is quite difficult to reconstruct the subjective biases and preconceived ideas underlying so many famous controversies in the history of music, and the fact that we are not able to ascertain wholly the viewpoints prevailing less than fifty years ago should teach us to be doubly cautious in passing judgment on contemporary phenomena.

By that time Mahler's *First Symphony* had had two rather inconsequential hearings, one in Budapest, another in Hamburg. Critics and audiences were slightly baffled, without showing much enthusiasm for or against this music. In the meantime Mahler prepared his *Second*, the so-called *Resurrection Symphony*. The landscape which he populated with his musical characters was still the picturesque German Middle Ages as seen through the eyes of the early German romanticists. The verses which Mahler had composed himself for his early songs, in a very curious process of literary anticipation, matched most completely in mood and content, vocabulary, inflexion and style, *Des Knaben Wunderhorn* (The Youth's Magic Horn), a collection of German folk-poems which Mahler did not know and use till years later.

Arnim and Brentano, the writers who had edited this collection in the beginning of the 19th century, were probably no more innocent than Mahler in their choice of inspiration. Be that as it may, this whole world of fair maidens and errant knights, forlorn sentinels and ghostly drummers, of moonlit castles and bewitched forests, of love's joy and sorrow, must have had relevant symbolical significance to those artists although much of it appears to us as dusty pasteboard settings and obsolete stage props. Mahler was beyond doubt perfectly candid in his musical interpretation of this literary substance. However, the intense excitement which still emanates from the music is due less to the faithfulness with which those romantic moods are given musical expression than to the desperation with which the composer clutches a set of ideas and emotions which were threatened by immediate disintegration. Evidence of this desperate nostalgia, which is one of the keynotes of Mahler's work, is furnished by the frequently exaggerated pathos of emotional expression, an almost spasmodic intensity of sentiment. Some commentators have found that this overheated eloquence betrays Mahler's Jewish origin. Without questioning the relative truth of such an explanation, the author is of the opinion that it too easily disposes of an essential spiritual aspect of Mahler's work in terms of a materialistic doctrine. Instead of penetrating to the core of a purely artistic problem, it obstructs unbiased discussion of what some people, rightly or wrongly, find irritating in Mahler's music.

Transitoriness and impending death are the standing topics of Mahler's musical discourse. The romantic scenery of *The Youth's Magic Horn* appears as embodiment of that which is inexorably doomed to perish. Just as Mahler chooses to associate his music with the picture of an archaic stage of life, so he clings to a musical idiom which is prevailingly pre-Wagnerian—that is, to a musical material which is not yet affected by the destructive principles let loose by Wagner against tonality. As mentioned before, this apparent regression is exactly what makes Mahler a propelling force in the evolution of music. It is his unconscious reaction against Wagner. In his late symphonies he succeeded in drawing the conclusions from this reaction and in laying down the foundations of the music to come.

If stylistic criteria are taken at face value, Mahler's early symphonies must appear strangely outdated even in relation to the time of their origin, considering that French impressionism was already about to strike a new and decidedly post-Wagnerian note. However, only the shape of the edifice and the material from which Mahler erected it are outdated; the cracks in the structure herald the future, and are the more obvious since shape and material are traditional. The real Mahler emerges where the symphonic form breaks down under the stress to which he had subjected it.

The passage just before the entrance of the chorus in the last movement of the *Second Symphony* is such a break; it is one of the most inspired and awesome pages of musical literature: when the horrifying silence is interrupted only by fearful tremors, as of frightened birds, and by the appalling calls of distant trumpets announcing the Last Judgment. This is not program music; it is not a musical illustration to a chapter of narrative. Music itself acts out its own agony, hopelessly witnessing the collapse of its overstrained structure.

Foretokens of Surrealism

Before his parents passed away in 1889, Mahler spent most of his vacations in Iglau. After the dissolution of the parental household he had no reason to return there any more. The considerable improvement of his financial situation enabled him to look for more attractive places than the dull Moravian town. In 1890 he traveled with his sister in Italy. After 1893, he spent the summers in Steinbach, on the lake of Atter, in the so-called Salzkammergut, a very beautiful country in Upper Austria, just east of Salzburg, that has its name from the important salt mines located there which were administrated in olden times by the archducal *chamber* (*Kammer*). Here wonderful lakes alternate with picturesque hills against the majestic background of the Northern slope of the Alps whose wild rocky ranges in this region carry such forbidding names as

Höllengebirge (Hell Mountains), *Totes Gebirge* (Death Mountains) and the like. The fact that Emperor Franz Joseph had his summer residence in Bad Ischl, one of the Salzkammergut resorts, had attracted many members of the nobility and *haute finance* to build their elegant summer homes in this section. An exciting juxtaposition of refined urbanism and romantic wilderness gave it a unique flavor. Although Mahler sought little contact with the metropolitan aspect of his environment, he certainly was enchanted by its manifest contrasts.

In those surroundings Mahler wrote his *Third Symphony* which is one of his most affirmative creations. It has been interpreted by himself as a comprehensive image of nature's immortality. And yet, the notion of death lurks even here, be it only in the recognition of man's transitoriness. Deep melancholy overcomes the musical poet as he watches the indifference of the universe towards humans and realizes that they participate in the unending life but for a little while. Again this melancholy is given eloquent expression through a symbol of bygone times: while the orchestra, in the soft sounds of high strings, seems to depict the dreamy silence of a summer night, we hear from far away the sentimental call of a postilion who blows his horn as the stagecoach moves quietly along. Again the material is neither novel nor original. The striking boldness of this and many similar passages lies in the fact that such apparently commonplace associations are used with the will to give voice to deep emotion and profound philosophical thought. The result is obtained by choosing first an obviously outworn, obsolete symbol, so that it appears as a quotation from another age and style, and by then placing it in a surprising context of grandeur and monumentality.

Seen from this angle, Mahler's style anticipates the basic principle of surrealism to an amazing extent. Doubtless Mahler was conscious of the extra-musical associations attached to many of his themes: children's songs, folk tunes, country dances, bugle calls, army marches and so forth. However, the associations never function according to the schedule of an extra-musical program, as they did in the Symphonic Poem of the Liszt and Strauss school. They function by their contrast to the immense symphonic context in which they appear. The opening motive of the *Third Symphony* is literally identical with the first phrase of a marching song which all Austrian school children used to sing. Produced by eight French horns playing at full blast in unison and placed in empty space, without any accompaniment, at the beginning of a symphonic movement of unheard-of dimensions, this motive takes on a very special significance precisely because of its being associated with that innocent little tune; a significance, however, that it would be difficult to analyze.

Mahler and Strauss

MAHLER DID NOT AROUSE NOTICEABLE ATTENTION as a composer until 1894 when his *First Symphony* was given another hearing in Weimar, at the instigation of Richard Strauss. This eminent composer (born only four years after Mahler) was at that time still interested in other people's music especially whenever such music seemed to corroborate his own doctrine of the programmatic *Symphonic Poem* without overshadowing his own accomplishments in this field. Thus, Mahler's symphony was labeled a *Symphonic Poem* and given the name *Titan,* after a novel of the German romanticist Jean Paul, as well as a suitable narrative program. Mahler accepted the promotional offices of Strauss with gratitude. It seems that he looked upon the younger colleague with a slightly exaggerated respect, which was possibly mixed with some envy of Strauss's more brilliant career. It was the understandable feeling of someone who had had to struggle hard throughout his life towards a man engaged in similar activities who had made so much faster headway. The difference between the two composers, however, was more essential than Mahler realized. Strauss is an author of extraordinary resourcefulness and unusual theatrical instinct. As a human being he took life more easily than Mahler, perhaps a reason why he is still alive while Mahler was called away from his work thirty years ago, having burned his candle at both ends. But it may also be the reason why Strauss appears today clearly as a figure of the faraway 19th century while Mahler's testament constantly generates new impulses, its inspiring problematical qualities being by no means exhausted.

Gustav Mahler Caricatured by Enrico Caruso

Mahler in Vienna
The Austrian Paradox

THE CULMINATING PERIOD IN MAHLER'S CAREER came when the dream of his life was realized: in the spring of 1897 he was first appointed conductor, shortly afterwards assistant to the director, and in the fall of the same year, director general of the Imperial Opera House in Vienna.

Every outstanding personality brought up in the peculiar intellectual atmosphere of Vienna lived ever after in a dialectical syncretism of love and hatred for that city which offered splendid potentialities for the highest accomplishments, as well as the most stubborn resistance to their realization. Vienna was the capital of an empire which, in the century of its most brilliant flowering, between 1680 and 1780 approximately, was a continental organism analogous to what the British Empire became in the 19th century on a world scale. However, the universality of the Austrian Empire was based on spiritual guidance rather than on administrative organization. The solution of the imperial problem —how to coordinate countless heterogeneous elements—was attempted by means of unanimity in the Catholic faith rather than on the principle of rational liberalism. Because of its Catholic orientation the Austrian Empire was suspected by liberals all over the world as a stronghold of sinister reaction and suppression; compared with more recent political phenomena, old Austria must appear as a paradise of peace and freedom, since Czechs and Poles, for instance, had permanent representatives in the cabinet and at times even prevailed in the government. How, if Austria had been what her foes pretended, could a Bohemian Jew have ruled with absolute power for ten years over the foremost artistic institution of the Empire?

The political decline of the Empire had begun with the exploits of Prussia under Frederick II, shortly after 1750. It was long concealed by the spectacular and unparalleled brilliance of cultural, and especially musical, life which had begun still earlier and continued until the beginning of the 20th century. Actually Mahler's exit from the opera house in 1907 marks the definite end of Vienna's musical supremacy. However, the feeling of the approaching decay was growing throughout the later 19th century, when the inability of coping with the increasing political difficulties on the part of the representatives of the imperial idea became more and more evident. A most peculiar attitude of hedonistic pessimism, joyful skepticism touching on morbid sophistication, became the dominant trait in Vienna's intellectual climate. And yet, the grand ideology of the Empire was still strong enough to bring forth scores of truly great artists and thinkers animated by the flame of universalism.

Their problem was how to reconcile ethical integrity, the attribute of any great personality, with the destructive cynicism which was the inescapable heritage of the generation. This dilemma is the simple explanation of the puzzling fact that the country which was famous for carefree street singers, sentimental waltzes and luscious pastry generated a goodly number of artists whose intellectual radicalism and ethical intransigency could well stand comparison with the fierce ruthlessness of medieval Spanish inquisitors. They developed the bewildering desire to be at odds with their period. Their inwardness and contempt of reality were sometimes alarming. A characteristic incident is related from Mahler's childhood. As somebody asked the boy what he would like to become when grown up he is reported to have answered: "A martyr."

Life in Vienna

Mahler's Conversion to Catholicism.

SOME TIME BEFORE MAHLER WAS CALLED TO Vienna, he accepted baptism and joined the Catholic Church. Gabriel Engel, Mahler's American biographer, intimates that this move was due to somewhat opportunistic considerations. "The mere suspicion," he writes, "that his lack of formal association with the church might be a hindrance (though he had never suffered from anti-semitism) caused him to go through the ritual of conversion to Catholicism. Thus if he were to meet with any obstacle it could not be that of creed." The author does not know on what evidence this interpretation is founded. But although Mahler may have given some cause for so materialistic an interpretation of his conversion, it was actually brought about by the inner logic of his evolution. His intimate and persistant relation to the subject of death is from the outset determined by the idea of redemption and personal immortality. Sometimes free-thinkers have claimed Mahler as one of their kind because of the "Pantheism" they read into his glorification of nature. To overlook Mahler's essentially dualistic philosophy, such bias is required as ill behooves a much vaunted liberal-mindedness. To the unprejudiced mind Mahler's work must appear as a most eloquent and consistent manifestation of Christian eschatology. The fact that the formalization of his religious allegiance coincided with his appointment at the Vienna Opera House merely proves that he integrated himself consciously with the idea of the Empire. If there was any opportunistic factor involved in his decision it was certainly the desire not to make his ultimate, inevitable defeat too easy for his adversaries. They should fight him on his own ground, not on a side issue.

And fight they did. The administrators of the Imperial Opera House seem at first to have feared the results of their own courage. They introduced Mahler, almost surreptitiously, into a subordinate position. It is quite characteristic that they were forced, through the sheer power of his presence, to enhance his position until he was endowed with unlimited power within a few months. One may safely assume that his adversaries started to fight him then and there, the very day on which they had yielded. From then on they would resent his superiority, that very quality for which they had needed him. Mahler's remarkable accomplishments during the following ten years are recorded on other pages of this book. To anyone who knows the conditions under which they had to be achieved, his final defeat appears self-evident; the only thing he marvels at is that it took ten long years to bring it about. It was the struggle of a perfectionist's iron will against the overwhelming array of inertia and indifference, connivance and stupidity, intellectual and moral decay. Mahler had to fail in the end.

Nevertheless, there were many satisfactions along the way. He had some excellent congenial collaborators at the opera house, and was hailed by public enthusiasm hardly conceivable elsewhere than in Vienna, where the affairs of the opera house used to be the permanent topics of popular discussion in street cars and grocery stores. Outwardly, Mahler's life was the life of a highly successful artist.

The remuneration which he received for his services was, according to the standards of the period, very handsome. In 1902 he founded a household of his own by marrying Alma Maria, the daughter of the late Jacob Emil Schindler, a fine painter and brilliant, though somewhat extravagant, personality of the late romantic epoch. Through the stepfather of his wife, the painter Karl Moll, Mahler came in contact with the modern movement in Fine Arts called *Secession.* Kolo Moser, Gustav Klimt, Egon Schiele, were remarkable painters belonging to this circle. A younger generation was represented by Adolf Loos, the great Austrian architect who had been in America and begun the promotion of ideas of the type later formulated by Frank Lloyd Wright, a most revolutionary venture forty years ago; Peter Altenberg, the poet, and Karl Kraus, the greatest satirist of the newer German literature and a true embodiment of the Austrian paradox mentioned before; Oskar Kokoschka, a leading figure in the oncoming expressionist movement; and many others. Of course, all progressive musicians of Vienna gathered enthusiastically around Mahler. The most important of his younger followers was Arnold Schönberg, Mahler's junior by fourteen years.

On the Threshold of "New" Music

DURING THE FIRST YEARS OF HIS VIENNA ENgagement, Mahler had completed his *Fourth Symphony*, his shortest and lightest symphonic work with curious allusions to Mozartian idiosyncrasies. For the last time he included a song from *The Youth's Magic Horn*, a delightful, naïve description of the eternal joys of heaven, as if borrowed from the illuminations of a medieval monkish manuscript: a tender, tentative outline of what might await us after death. Another work of this period, dealing with the tragic aspect of death, is a song cycle called *Kindertotenlieder*, one of Mahler's most intimate and moving compositions. It is a telling illustration of the fact that the great artist anticipates, or substitutes for, experience by divinatory imagination. Anyone who knows that Mahler was actually bereaved of one of his two children will be inclined to think that the unusual expressive power of these songs comes out of the profound grief caused by the tragic loss. In fact, the songs were written years before the sad event occurred. The first period of Mahler's work is closed.

The *Fifth Symphony*, completed in 1902, opens a new cycle and indicates a great inner crisis. No other work by Mahler underwent so many revisions from the hand of its maker as this one. In 1911, Mahler wrote "I cannot understand how I could have at that time written so much like a beginner. Clearly the routine I had acquired in the first four symphonies deserted me altogether, as if a totally new message demanded a new technique." If nothing else, this experience alone would prove Mahler's legitimation as a truly creative genius. It is the stigma of mediocre minds that they persist in acquired routines while the genius is distinguished by being receptive to new messages that seem to sway him completely from his course.

The strange feeling of being lost which Mahler experienced in writing his *Fifth Symphony* was due to the fact that he had entered upon the territory of the "new" music of the 20th century, a style which was thus far forecast in his work only by indirection. However, no essential change in the character of his ideas had occurred. They still had the unique flavor of "quotation." But their purely musical treatment becomes different. They are once more removed from their original context in that they are greatly reduced to melodic lines. The harmonic background of those perfectly tonal ideas becomes very tenuous and is at times discarded entirely. Instead a curiously ruthless contrapuntal technique holds sway. This is neither the retrospective counterpoint of Max Reger, which frequently sounds like inflated Bach, nor the glittering texture of Richard Strauss which is mostly animated harmony. It is a new kind of genuine polyphony; all commentators on Mahler, even skeptical ones, agree that therein lies his unique and all-important contribution to the evolution of our contemporary music.

In view of the demands of his functions at the opera house, Mahler's musical output in these years appears quite prodigious. After the *Fifth Symphony* in 1902 he completed the *Sixth* in 1904, the *Seventh* in 1905, all three being compositions of tremendous dimensions. How they acted as catalyst in the critical stage of the musical language at that time is shown by the fact they were followed in 1908 by those utterly revolutionary *Three Piano Pieces* by Arnold Schönberg which threw open the door to the vast and still unconquered field of atonality. Debussy and Scriabin had gone farther in the dismemberment and the transformation of the tonal vocabulary than Mahler who remained faithful to his *montage* of "quotations." However, it is probably just this fixation on obsolete thematic material that induced him to elaborate his new contrapuntal methods, and these methods were precisely the factor which determined the direction of the most progressive trend in music to the present day.

It is reported that Mahler did not approve particularly of the early atonal exploits of Schönberg and his disciples. This may well be the case since it is quite frequently not possible for an innovator to grasp fully the implication of his venture into the unknown. He may sometimes even be unaware of having opened a new avenue, and put greater emphasis on elements of his invention that seem to link him to the past rather than to the future. One has also to consider that Mahler witnessed only a few of the first tentative moves in the new territory. At any rate it is certain that no other group gave more enthusiastic testimony of their indebtedness to Gustav Mahler than the new Viennese school.

Mahler Leaves Vienna

AFTER 1900 MAHLER USED TO SPEND HIS VAcations at Mayernigg on the Wörthersee in Carinthia. When his eldest daughter died there in 1907 at the age of five, he could not bear the sad memories associated with this place and went for the remaining summers of his life to Alt-Schluderbach near Toblach in the Dolomite Mountains of Southern Tyrol (now in Italy and called Dobbiacco). Because of his ailing heart, he was not able any longer to enjoy the magnificent scenery by taking long walks or climbing mountains as he had used to do in earlier days. The passionate longing with which he must have looked on the jagged peaks and the multicolored domes of the Dolomites, towering high above the green immensity of forests and meadows, went into the *Lied von der Erde* and the *Ninth Symphony*, which he wrote in Alt-Schluderbach, and impregnated these works with the burning melancholy of renouncement, resignation and farewell. Mahler did not live to see the completion of the beautiful summer house which he had planned to build for himself at the famous Semmering heights, a few hours south of Vienna, from blueprints which he had brought back from America. His widow carried out the project and resided there during many summers, making the house a most hospitable center of all creative and intellectual activities in the last decades of Austria. Artists and scientists of all branches, politicians of all color shades, gathered there and engaged in highly stimulating discussions.

It is quite characteristic that several different stories are told about the immediate cause of Mahler's resignation from the directorship of the Vienna Opera House. Too many people apparently were interested in concealing the truth that no meritorious reason for removing Mahler from his office existed. The different versions based on gossip and surmise agree at least in one point: that petty and ignominious stratagems were used to bring about Mahler's fall. Whatever may have been the final cause, Mahler's time was up. He left the place of his highest triumphs victorious: he had demonstrated to what unbelievable degree inert matter could be animated by fiery spirit.

Mahler's valedictory note to the staff of the opera

house, a document of exemplary dignity, was torn down from the bulletin board by barbarous hands the moment he had left his post. The wreckers rushed from the wings in which they had waited impotently for so long. They set out at once to destroy what Mahler had built. But even in the late 'twenties, the Vienna Opera House was still capable of some remarkable effort; everyone knew that all that was praiseworthy was due to the man who had been driven out twenty years before.

Mahler and America

TODAY IT IMPRESSES US AS SYMBOLIC THAT Mahler should have directed his steps to that part of the world that was later to become the refuge of so many of his kind: America. The tremendous exodus of the catastrophic 'thirties only seems to be caused by different reasons; what happened to Mahler was actually but a foretoken of the formidable upheaval of arrogant mediocrity that in these times chastises mankind the world over. In America, Mahler refrained from burdening himself with managerial duties at the Metropolitan Opera in New York, a position which had been offered to him; instead he conducted there only a limited number of performances and devoted most of his labor to the reorganization of the New York Philharmonic Orchestra. The task was very pleasing to him since he had always regretted not having as much time for concert work as he would have liked. Alas, he was not to enjoy for long his activities in the refreshing atmosphere of the New World. His health was definitely broken. When he returned to Vienna after his first season in America, physicians gave him hope for any considerable extension of his life only on the condition that he give up all strenuous work. But this was advice he would not heed.

Before Mahler left the Vienna Opera House in 1907, he had completed his most spectacular work, the *Eighth Symphony*. Together with the following opus, *Das Lied von der Erde*, it forms a new group of symphonies in which the vocal element again is present, even prevailing to an unprecedented extent. While the *Eighth Symphony*, designed for a huge orchestra and an immense chorus, spells majestic beauty and transfigured joy, *Das Lied von der Erde*, a symphonic cycle of songs for two solo voices, is the epitome of sadness, melancholy and resignation. It was written after Mahler had learned that he was doomed. No matter how wonderful and effective these works may be, the one because of the array of sonorous quantity, the strategical mastery of handling of such masses and the irresistible *élan* of its enthusiasm, the other through the heart-rending intensity of sorrowful introspection, they can not match the *Ninth Sym-*

phony, Mahler's last completed work, in regard to prophetic significance in purely musical terms. Here Mahler stands once more upon the mysterious threshold beyond which lies a new unexplored province of the realm of music. Mahler's "quotation" themes appear as ghostly symbols, reduced to bare outlines; the texture is thinned out, much as in some passages of the latest Beethoven; the independent melodic entities are projected bluntly against a vast empty horizon and clash with each other in harsh, portentous friction. This is not only Mahler's last symphony: the symphonic form as such is torn apart after having been tried to the limit.

Anyone who looks upon the evolution of music with an unbiased mind will admit that all further attempts to carry on with the traditional symphonic form have been of an epigonous character. If this form is to live on and to thrive again, a fresh start has to be made. Indications of such a new beginning may be found in the various forms of "chamber symphonies" which were written in the 'twenties after Schönberg had shown the way with his *Kammersymphonie*. The huge orchestral apparatus is replaced by small combinations of solo instruments, the over-extended form gives way to extremely condensed structures. Although the external appearance of those works seems the opposite of Mahler's symphonic ideal, they are essentially indebted to his exploits in their emphasis on rich contrapuntal construction.

The first wave of general acknowledgment of Mahler's compositions in Europe came shortly after the first World War, inaugurated by the Mahler Festival of 1920 in Amsterdam. After that, there was for many years hardly a concert season in Vienna, or Berlin, or other major music center in Europe that did not include performances of several of Mahler's symphonies. It was, and still is, different in America, partly because of the peculiar influence exerted here by Jan Sibelius, Mahler's junior by only five years. If one wants to ascertain the exact position of Mahler's work and to sound out its significance in the present situation of music, it is worthwhile to pause here for a moment and to examine his relation to Sibelius. It was pointed out before that Mahler's symphonies are based on thematic material which is greatly made up from "familiar" stuff. In view of the well-known attitude of average audiences, one would expect that this fact would be the cause of marked popularity. The reason why this is not so is the alarming context into which the familiar material is brought, by virtue of disconcerting contrapuntal combinations and oversized dimensions. The shock reaction thus produced is akin to that caused by certain surrealistic devices which show the familiar living-room through a distorting magnifying glass, as it were, and thus reveal it as a horror chamber.

No such disturbing impressions emanate from Sibelius's symphonies. His idiom is what some people praise and others snub as "moderately modern"; that is to say that, on the one hand, it lacks Mahler's dialectical relation to a lost musical world and, on the other hand, does not imply the forward pointing conclusions to be drawn from such dialectics. In the light of the viewpoints set forth in this study, Sibelius appears in his relation to Mahler in a position similar to Bruckner's at his time. The Finnish composer, too, is a man of great natural simplicity of mind, endowed with profound poetic sensitivity. He also is a thinking musician, and the various original ways in which he approached the symphonic form show clearly that he has been mindful of the artistic problems involved. However, despite the relative merits of his accomplishments, these efforts seem historically somewhat belated in view of the more progressive solutions offered by Mahler. Sibelius is a legitimate heir of the symphonic tradition in that he exhibits some of the magnitude of gesture so characteristic of the old symphony. He does so, however, by renouncing almost completely the contrapuntal pithiness of texture which was Mahler's fateful contribution to the problem of the symphonic form. Absence of textural complication and of straightforward thematic statements lend Sibelius's style a sort of bleakish, faint luster appealing to listeners who understand by symphonic style a distinguished musical display of soft-pedaled emotionalism (the factor of dignified distinction having been ushered in especially by Brahms, Cesar Franck and related composers). The great respect in which everything national is nowadays held has enhanced Sibelius's popularity, since the idiosyncrasies of his music have been rationalized as being particularly expressive of the character of the Finnish people and landscape. If that means provincialism (as opposed to the all-embracing universalism which animated the classical symphony), it can more conclusively be explained by the limitations of Sibelius's musical outlook than by arbitrary associations with extra-musical elements, race, landscape, and the like. Just appreciation of Mahler would by no means imply belittling Sibelius. Passing judgment on the magnitude of talent possessed by great artists and playing one up to the detriment of another is a futile entertainment of immature minds. Prospects of a re-birth in America of thinking and feeling on a world scale rather than in terms of narrow nationalistic concepts coincide with the hope for a more adequate evaluation of Mahler's significance than he has hitherto enjoyed. The attitude of some younger musicians in this country seems to hold promises in this direction. Thus Mahler's frequent remark "My time has yet to come" has a particularly prophetic ring as far as America is concerned.

Exit

DURING THE SEASON 1910–1911 MAHLER WAS forced to curtail his concert obligations in America because of his rapidly declining health. At the end of February 1911 he hurried to Paris in order to undergo an emergency treatment. It was of no avail. He had only the desire to spend his last hours in Vienna, the city for which he felt that strange mixture of love and hatred, an infatuation shared by so many of his kind. He reached the place of his triumphs just in time and passed away on May 18, 1911. Great crowds attended his funeral at the cemetery of Grinzing, little conscious of the guilt which the city of Vienna had contracted in torturing the deceased genius.

The fundamental feature of Mahler's music is the army march, running the whole gamut from the triumphal cortege to the muffled sounds of the funeral service. Writers on Mahler found an easy explanation for this in the fact that Mahler passed his childhood near the army barracks of Iglau and used to watch the drills of the Austrian soldiery which were accompanied by unusually beautiful bugle calls. The author believes that such vital artistic phenomena are not adequately explained by this primitive interplay of cause and effect. Mahler as an artist was impersonated energy, conscious of the dynamic character of his musical mission; and he was a fighter. No wonder that his propensity for striking symbols made him choose again and again the martial rhythm of bugle and drum.

During his last days in New York, Mahler was working on the sketches for his *Tenth,* never finished, *Symphony.* When the author was entrusted with the task of editing two almost complete movements of this work, he was told that Mahler found himself inspired to a very strange solo on the bass drum by the music that accompanied a New York fireman's funeral which he had observed from his hotel window. It sounds like isolated gun discharges, far, far away. Mahler was spared hearing the real gun fire that was to din in the ears of mankind so soon after his departure. Safe from all trouble, the great Austrian soldier of music, intrepid sentinel and *avant-garde,* rests from his tireless onward marching, amidst the glorious vineyards of Grinzing, until the trumpet of the Last Judgment, so familiar to his divining mind, shall call him to everlasting salvation.

Poughkeepsie, N. Y.
May–June 1941

NOTE

For the factual data on Gustav Mahler's life I am particularly indebted to Guido Adler's *Gustav Mahler*, Universal Edition, Vienna 1916; Gabriel Engel's *Gustav Mahler, Song-Symphonist*, New York 1932; and Paul Stefan's *Gustav Mahler:* A Study of his Personality and Work, New York, 1913.

E. K.

Index

A

Abbey, St. Florian, 162
absentminded look, 143
absentmindedness, 15
Ablösung im Sommer, 94
Abschied, Der, 59, 124
Absolute music, 69, 133
Academy of Music, Imperial, 159
Adler, 220
Aida, 17
Alberich, 67
"All against all," 61, 120
Allgemeine Deutsche Musikverein, 3
All-Eternal Mother, 151
Aliosha, Ivan and, 139
Alma Maria, 202
Alps, 191
Altenberg, Peter, 203
Alt-Schluderbach, 208
America, 10, 52, 106, 170, 182, 203, 209, 211, 214, 216, 217, 218
American biographer, Mahler's, 200
Amsterdam, 214
Andante, Beethoven's, 134
  Mozart's, 134
Andrei, 123
Angels, forty thousand, 85
"Angel Movement," 116
Angelus Silesius, 137
animals, 132
Anselmus, 7
Anti-Wagnerianism, 136
Anti-Wagnerites, 167
antisemitism, 200
Anthony's Sermon to the Fish, St., 16
Antonius von Paduas Fischpredigt, 94
Apollo, 103
Archangel, 78
Argonauts, 159
Argus, 86
Aristotle, 136
Arnim-Brentano, 92, 188
artistic gospel, new, 181
artists, 37, 38

art of the eye, 140
arts, fine, 203
"Arise, Arise, my Heart!", 111
Ascende lumen, 58
atonal exploits, 207
atonality, 206
atomic theory, 135
Atter, Lake of, 191
Attersee, 22, 30
Auenburgerstrasse, 45
Aus! Aus!, 93
Austria, 198
  Upper, 161, 166, 191
Austrian, 157
Austrian architect, 203
Austrian character, 90
Austrian composers, 160
Austrian dialect, 100
  Empire, 198
  manner, 100
  military music, 100
  monarch, 167
  paradox, 197, 203
  phenomenon, 163
  soldiery, 219
  schoolchildren, 193
  Tyrol, 57
  waltz, 100
"Austrianity," 157
avant-garde, 219

B

Bach, 102, 126, 160, 206
Bad Hall, 166, 167
Bad Ischl, 192
bands, Vienna's military, 100
baptism, 200
barber, French, 62
Barnum & Bailey, 56
Bayreuth, 159, 164, 168, 181
beat, exemplary, 79
  accuracy of his, 79
  seemingly simple, 86
"Beautiful is difficult," 142
Beckmesser, 68, 71
Beethoven, 37, 58, 77, 80, 81, 84, 89, 90, 98, 110, 126, 134, 142, 167, 177, 213
Beethovenesque greatness, 107
Beethoven-nearness, 81
Beethoven Prize, 167
Beethoven's Soul, 81, 82
  symphonic utterances, 177
Being, eternal, rigid, 113
  and Doing, 134
  Supreme, 164
Bellini's images, 133
beloved Earth, 151
Berlin, 19, 20, 23, 29, 32, 168, 214
Berlioz, 90, 115
Beyond, the, 133
  the World, 134
Biblical oratorios, 133
birth, Gustav's, 158
"Birth of Tragedy," 109
"birth of light, fair is the," 78
Boehler, 85
Boieldieu, 39
Bone, The Singing, 91
Bohemia, 162
  Southern, 158
Bohemian, German-, 91
Bohemian, 157, 159, 198
Brahms, 103, 167, 186, 216
Brahms' opinion, 187
Brahmsian lyricism, 187
Brentano, Arnim and, 92, 188
Brothers in Apollo, 103
  Karamazoff, 139

Bruckner, 58, 90, 99, 142, 160, 161, 163, 215
Bruckner's analogous trend, 163
  compositions, 165
  disciple, 164
  style, 163
  work, 163
Budapest, 179, 182, 183, 185, 186, 187
bugle-calls, 193
Bülow, Hans von, 168, 186, 187
Bülow's tactless behavior, 170
  conscience, 168
  death, 186

C

Callot, Funeral March, 3, 106
canon, prowling, 106
"Cantata," 167
cantos, six, 123
caricatures, 85
Carinthia, 208
catalyst, 206
Catherine, 76
Catholic, 164
  Church, 200
  German, 161
  faith, 198
  orientation, 198
Catholicism, 200
Century, *15th*, 8
  19th, 158, 188, 196, 197, 199
  20th, 163, 205
Cervantes, 26, 139
chalk-scratchings, 71
"Chamber symphonies," 213
Charpentier, 39
children, 16, 204
children's choir, 58
  songs, 193
Chinese lyric art, 147
Chinese poems, 151
Christian eschatology, 201
classic, 88, 98
classical, 98, 99, 102, 156, 216
coffee-house, 35, 45, 61
Cologne, 47
composer's cottage, 25, 61
"Concerto," Giorgione's, 7, 42, 133
contrapuntal, combinations, 214
  construction, 214
  mastery, 102, 125
  methods, 207
  pithiness, 215
  style, 101
  technique, 206
  work, 102
conversation (s), 6, 27, 46, 47, 50, 56, 60, 61, 119, 137, 138, 141–3
conversion, 200
Coriolanus, 81
cosmic idea, 141
  phenomenon, 139
costume, 73, 86
counterpoint, 162, 206
Countess, 69, 70
country dances, 193
"Creator Spiritus," 58, 121, 150
criteria, stylistic, 189
criticism, self, 159
critics, 23
Crown (Hungarian), 179
Czech farmers, 158
  names, 156
  settlement, 158

Czechoslovakia, 158
Czechs, 198

D

Dalibor, 30
Das Gesindel, 113
Das irdische Leben, 95
Das klagende Lied, 88, 91, 167, 168
Das Lied von der Erde, 54, 58, 123, 124, 147, 151, 153, 208, 212
Debussy, 206
"dear Earth," 60, 152
death, 54, 58, 94, 120, 129, 150, 151, 152, 186, 189, 192, 200
"Death Mountains," 192
demoniac nature, 16, 94, 131
  obsession, 6
deification of nature, 148
"Der Mahler!", 35
Der Schildwache Nachtlied, 94, 101
Der Siebenkäs, 138
Der Sommer marschiert ein, 101, 112, 113
Der Tambourgesell, 93, 101
Des Antonius von Padua Fischpredigt, 94
Des knaben Wunderhorn, 92, 188
"desultory," 13
devoutness, 133
dialectical syncretism, 197
Die drei Pintos, 171
"Die I shall only to live," 111
Die zwei blauen Augen von meinem Schatz, 95
digitalis, 63
Dionysian saturation, 28, 148
Dionysius, 148
disease, 132
Divine Love, 116
Divine Service, 133
divinatory imagination, 204
divining mind, 220
Divinity, spirit of, 133
Djamilehx, 30
Dobbiacco, 57, 208
Domestica, Sinfonia, 86
Don Giovanni, 40, 74
Don Quixote, 26
Dostoievsky, 139
drama, 69, 70, 72, 73, 75
dramatic characters, 178
  composer, 177, 178
  conflicts, 178
  directions, 71
  element, 177
  events, 71
  expression, 70, 96
  feeling, 96, 178
  function, 74
  intentions, 70
  -musical, 72
  performances, 72, 73
  presentation, 70
  side, 178
  situation, 72
  vehicle, 183
dynamics, 79

E

Earth, dear, 60, 151, 152
Earth, 123, 134
  beloved, 151
earthworm, 136
eagle, 61
Eckermann, 137
Eighth Symphony, 45, 46, 57, 102, 121, 150, 212
élan, 212

Elsa, 68, 69
Emperor, 42, 192
Empire, 158, 167, 168, 197, 198, 199, 201
  British, 197
End of the World, 20
endemic naïveté, 163
English, opera in, 182
Engel, Gabriel, 200, 220
entelechian teaching, 136
ensemble, 79
Ensemble, Mysterym, 69
Epoch, First, 146, 147
  Second, 146, 149
  Third, 147
  romantic, 202
  "temporal," 149
Ernest, Duke of Swabia, 159
Es sungen drei Engel, 94
E. T. A. Hoffmann, 16, 138, 166
Eternal Mother, 151
ethical integrity, 199
  intransigency, 199
ethics, 143
Eugen Onegin, 30
Europe, 214
European universities, 162
Evil, World-, 132
exactitude, 80
exactness, 79
experiment, 74
expressionist movement, 203

F

"Fair is the birth of light," 78
fairy-tale, 63, 91, 117
fairy-tale-like, 6
Falk, 137
fanatic, 16, 169
fanaticism, 40
fanatical adjuration, 86
farewell letter, 44
Faust, 78, 121, 122, 125, 147, 150, 152
Faustian man, 134, 150
Fechner, 135
Festival, Mahler, 214
  Musicians', 3
  Music, 47
Fidelio, 40, 54, 81
Figaro, 69, 71, 72, 76
Fifth Symphony, 45, 47, 99, 101, 102, 104, 119, 120, 125, 150, 205, 206
Finnish composer, 215
  people, 216
first four symphonies, 205
First Symphony, 16, 95, 98, 100, 105, 106, 108, 110, 118, 123, 137, 173, 187, 195
first World War, 214
Fish, St. Anthony's Sermon to the, 16
Fischpredigt, Des Antonius von Padua, 94
Flood, Mrs., 68
"flower mood," 114
Flying Dutchman, 30
"folk-like," 91
folk-poems, 188
folk-poetry, 90, 91, 188
folk-song, 90, 98
folk-tunes, 193
form, symphonic, 89, 97, 137, 164, 190, 213, 216
four-hands, 18
four-handed piano, 20
Fourth Symphony, 45–48, 95, 99–101, 103, 116–119, 146, 204
Franck, Cesar, 216

Franz Joseph, 42, 192
Frederick II, 198
free-thinkers, 201
Freischütz, 39
French horns, 193
  impressionism, 190
Frenchman, ingenious, 90
Fricka, 11
fugue, art of the, 102
Funeral, 64
  fireman's, 219
  march, 95, 101, 119, 137
  March in the Manner of Callot, 3, 106
  Music, 14
  Service, 108, 218, 219

G

gaiety, 18, 116
"Gay Science," 116
genius, 174, 186, 205
German, 157, 158
  -Bohemian, 91
  centers, 158
  Catholic, 161
  folk-poems, 188
  literature, 203
  Middle Ages, 187
  musicians, 156
  nation, 181
  Opera House, 170
  romanticist (s), 187, 195
Germans, 158
Germany, 14, 168
Germanic top layer, 167
Gesänge guter Laune, 95
Gesindel, Das, 113
Giorgione, 7, 42, 133
Giorgione's vision, 8
Gluck, 39, 75, 77
God, faith in, 162
God-seeker, 150
Goethe, 121, 130, 135, 137, 160
Goethe's conversations, 137
  pronouncement, 150
Goetz, 39, 76, 77
Götterdämmerung, 14
Great Recall, 101, 111
gradations, symphonic, 120
Grimm, 91
Grinzing, 61, 64, 218, 220
grotesque, 88, 90, 113
growth, lust-impelled, 113
Gutmann, Emil, 56
Gymnasium, 158

H

Händel, 160
Halevy, 39
Hall, Bad, 166, 167
Hamburg, 10, 15, 19, 29, 60, 86, 136, 185, 187
  Symphony Orchestra, 186
  Opera, 4, 14
  Stadttheater, 21
  Theater, 15
Hanoverische-Münden, 168
Hänsel und Gretel, 5
Hanslick, 167
Hans von Grethe, 91
Hans Sachs, 68
harmony with the infinite, 122
Hartmann, 137
haute finance, 192
Haydn, 100, 103, 114, 117
Haydn Variations, 103
headache, 20
health, 179, 212, 218
heart, 49, 53, 68, 87, 89, 119, 143, 145, 150, 152, 208
Heaven, 117
Heavenly Life, 117

Hell Mountains, 192
Hessia, 169
Himmlische Leben, 94
Hoelderlin, 137
Höllengebirge, 24, 192
Hoffmann, E. T. A., 4, 16, 166
Hoffmann, Tales of, 37, 77, 138
Hofoper, 29, 36, 54
Hofoperntheater, 41
"home," 63
Hrabanus Maurus, 121
humor, 23, 62, 93, 99, 129, 132
humorous songs, 94
Humperdinck, 6
Hungarian, 183
Hungarian-speaking, 180
  Operas in, 182
hymns, 122

I

"I," 83, 84
"I am a musician," 153
Ich atmet einen Lindenduft, 96
Ich bin der Welt abhanden gekommen, 96
idea, musical, 97
  symphonic, 89, 120
ideas, tonal, 206
Iglau, 168, 191, 219
illness, acute, 153
immortality, 192, 201
imagination, divinatory, 204
"incorrigible revolutionary," 187
inquisitors, Spanish, 199
insidious illness, 62
instrumentation, 27, 47, 48, 56, 80, 90, 96, 103, 104, 120, 123
integration, 180–182
"Interesting is easy," 142
interests, multiplicity of, 140
intellectual climate, Vienna's, 199
"intermittent loyalty," 144
interpretation, 69, 75, 77, 78, 80, 81, 83, 84, 87, 126, 188
interpreters, 174, 175, 181, 183
inventiveness, Weber's, 172
inventive work, 97
invention, musical, 97, 99, 107, 123, 124, 206
Iphigenia, 40, 75
irdische Leben, Das, 95
Italian operatic music, 11
Italy, 57, 191, 208

J

Jammer der Erde, Trinklied vom, 122
Jean Paul, 85, 137, 138, 166, 195
Jew, Bohemian, 157, 159
Jews, 157, 158, 198
Jewess (La Juive), 39, 77
Jewish boy, 162
  intellectuality, 162
  minority, 158
  origin, Mahler's, 189
Jihlava, 158
jokes, 139
Judgement, Last, 101, 111, 190, 220

K

Kalist, 158
Kammersymphonie, 213
Kapellmeister, 158, 185
  Musik, 186
  Kreisler, 4
  first, 30
Karamazoff, Brothers, 139
Kaspar, 39
Kassel, 169, 172
Kindertotenlieder, 96, 204
King Henry, 53
klagende Lied, Das, 88, 91, 167, 168
Klopfstock, 111
Klimt, Gustav, 203
Knaben Wunderhorn, Des, 92, 188
Kokoschka, Oskar, 203
Krauss, Karl, 203

L

Landestheater, 56
Last Judgement, 101, 111, 190, 220
Laibach, 167, 168
lansquenet romanticism, 90, 91
  manners, 92
Leipzig, 170, 171, 172, 173, 179
Leonore Overture, 81
letter (s), 22, 44, 52, 106, 143, 148, 152, 153
liberalism, 198
liberal-mindedness, 201
liberals, 198
license, ingenious, 75
  interpretative, 77
Lied von der Erde, Das, 54, 58, 123, 124, 147, 151, 153, 208, 212
Lieder eines fahrenden Gesellen, 88, 91, 95, 172, 173
Liedlein erdacht, Wer hat dies, 95
light, Fair is the birth of, 78
Light, Primordial, 110, 111
lighting, 73, 86
Lindhorst, Archivarius, 7
Liszt, 193
Little Recall, 117
Ljubliana, 167
Loge, 11
Lohse, Otto, 10
Lohengrin, 30, 53, 68, 69
Loos, Adolf, 203
Lord's Prayer, 154
Lotze, 135
love, almighty, 119
Love, Divine, 116
Löwe, 21
lyric art, Chinese, 147
lyricisms, Brahmsian, 187

M

Madonna, 133
Magic Flute, 40
Magic Horn, Youth's, 92, 93, 115, 185, 188, 189, 204
Mahler, Bernhard, 157
  Festival, 214
  Marie, 157
Mahler's accomplishments, 202
  activity, 40, 171
  advent, 42
  adversaries, 51
  American biographer, 200
  authority, 173
  appearance, 8
  brother, 18

Mahler's accomplishments (*Continued*)
- brothers, 157
- career, 197
- childhood, 199
- classical tendencies, 102
- compositions, 110, 157, 167
  - earlier, 95, 186
  - most intimate, 204
- conducting, 85, 86
- contact with intellectual matters, 139
- contribution, fateful, 216
- contribution, last, 173
- conversion, 200
- creations, 21, 47
- creative work, 27, 88, 124
- daring, 90
- demands, 11
- dialectical relation, 215
- direction, 86
- discourse, musical, 189
- disdain of applause, 145
- dramatic gifts, 67
- dualistic philosophy, 201
- emotion, 112
- employers, 174
- example, 30
- exit, 198
- fondness for Jean Paul, 137
- frequent remark, 213
- genealogical tree, 89
- genius, 174, 186
- heart, 49, 68
- imagination, 110, 157
- ideas, 181
- idealistic philosophy, 201
- influence, 9
- innovation, 182
- instigation, 10
- intellectual interests, 141

Mahler's accomplishments (*Continued*)
- instrumentation, art of, 103
- knowledge, acquisition of, 140
- life, 108, 202
- legitimation, 205
- management, 183
- manner, 5
- marches, 100
- mind, masterful, 41
  - presence of, 43
- Mozart, last performances, 186
- music, 9, 163, 167, 189, 218
- musical output, 206
- nature, 20, 42, 106, 146
  - essential, 91, 93
- operatic deeds, 169
- outbursts, impulsive, 13
- patience, 5
- personality, 5, 160
- presentations, 76
- principles, general, 182
- qualities, superior, 186
- Rheingold, 11
- repertoire, 39
- resignation, 209
- relationship, 148
- religious inclinations, 134
- senior, 159
- services, 180
- significance, 216
- silence, 51
- sisters, 157
- songs, 90, 91, 93, 97
- soul, 94, 118, 134
- superiors, 168, 170
- symphonic ideal, 213
- symphonies, 177, 187, 189, 195, 213, 214

Mahler's accomplishments (*Continued*)
  style, 193
  task, 42
  testament, 196
  testimony, 110
  thematics, 90
  time, 209
  tunes, 163
  valedictory, 209
  vision, 82
  widow, 209
  work, last completed, 213
  works, 47, 189, 201, 205, 214
  world-sorrow, 139
Mahleresque, 124
man in the street, 183
managerial duties, 214
Mannheim, 77
manysidedness, 140, 141
march, 101
marches, 100, 193
march melodies, 18
marching song, 193
martyr, 199
Marzellini's suit, 76
Mayernigg, 208
Meistersinger, 12
Mediterranean, 82
melancholy, 128, 192, 209, 212
Merry Wives of Windsor, 77
metaphysical perception, 140
  problems, 60
  question (s), 46, 118, 119, 120
  urge, 150
Metropolitan, 55, 211
Mickiewicz, 148
microcosm, 135
Middle Ages, German, 187
Midnight Poem, 115
Miracle!, 53
misunderstanding, 31, 143, 149
Mitternacht, Um, 95
"moderately modern," 215
modulation, 89, 90
Moll, Karl, 202
mood, flower, 114
moods, Panic, 113
  romantic, 188
money, 144
Monteverdi, 180
Moravia, 60, 158, 167, 191
Moser, Kolo, 203
Mother, All-Eternal, 151
movement, symphonic, 122, 193, 194
Mozart, 39, 43, 71, 74, 76, 77, 177
Mozart's orchestra, 74
  Andante, 134
Mozartian idiosyncrasies, 204
Mrs. Flood, 68
Munich, 47, 56, 57
murder, 132
Music, Society of the Friends of, 159
  evolution of, 213
  history of, 187
  "New," 204, 205
  Spirit of, 109
musical re-creation, 83, 84
  supremacy, Vienna's, 198
Musician, Unknown, 90
  symphonic, 111
Musicians, Society of Creative, 47
musico-dramatic style, 181

musicological continuity, 104
musicologists, 162
Musikverein, 49
Mystics, The, 137
"My time has yet to come," 217

N

Nachtlied, Der Schildwache, 94, 101
naïveté, endemic, 163
Nana, 135
Nature, 132
"nature-lover," 28
Neumann, Angelo, 170
"New" Music, 204, 205
New World, 212
New York, 55, 56, 59, 62, 211, 219
New York Philharmonic, 211
Nibelungen, 12
Nicht Wiedersehen, 95
Nietzsche, 109, 115, 133, 136
Nikisch, Arthur, 171
Nile, 113
Ninth Symphony (Beethoven), 89
Ninth Symphony (Mahler), 54, 58, 59, 80, 100, 102, 103, 125, 147, 151, 153, 208, 212, 213
"No," 120
non placet, 120
nocturnal, the, 88, 139
  element, 93, 131
  music, 115
  piece, 99
  pieces, three, 121
  round, 94
  side, 138
nocturnal (*Continued*)
  vision, 83
Nordic Symphony, 91, 159

O

oats, wild, 149
oddity, 149
Olmütz, 167, 168
Olomouc, 167
omnipotence, 132
Onegin, Eugen, 30
opera, 34, 42–45, 49, 50, 52, 54, 55, 70, 87, 176, 182
Opera, Berlin, 29, 32, 168, 170
  Budapest, 179, 183
  Hamburg, 4, 5, 14
  Leipzig, 179
  Prague, 170
Opera, Riga, 31
  Vienna, 8, 15, 29–34, 36, 41, 55, 146, 149, 197, 201, 202, 209, 210, 212
opera house, impeccable, 180
opera in English, 182
  in Hungarian, 182
operatic music, Italian, 11
operettas, 166
Orchestra, Berlin Philharmonic, 19
  Vienna Philharmonic, 19, 20, 37, 49
Ortrud, 68
"other man," 83, 84
Otto, 18

P

Pan, 148
Panic moods, 113
  movement, 148
Pan erwacht, 112, 113
Pantheism, 201

Pantheist, 148
Parcae, 60
Paris, 20, 56, 62, 218
Parsifal, 112, 168
Patmos, 137
perfectionist's iron will, 202
Petersburg, 144
Petrucchio, 76
Pfitzner, 39
Phaeacian, 35
Phantastique, Symphonie, 115
Philharmonic, Vienna, 19, 20, 37, 49
  Berlin, 19
Philistines, 12, 62
Piano Pieces, Three (Schönberg), 206
  lessons, 166
  songs, 91
Pizarro, 67
Poem, Symphonic, 193, 195
Poles, 198
political change, 180
  constellation, 180
  decline, 198
  phenomena, 198
Pollini, 4, 19, 21
post-Wagnerian, 189
Pot, Golden, 7
Prague, 56, 170
Prayer, the Lord's, 154
precision, 80
premieres, 46–48
Pressburg, 29–31, 68
"pre-stabilized harmony," 71
pre-Wagnerian, 189
Primordial Light, 110, 111
problematics of style, 114
program music, 105, 108, 110, 190, 193
programs, 144, 145, 165
Promethean descent, 127
prophetic significance, 213
provincialism, 216
Proteus, 84
Prussia, 198
Prussian Court Theater, 168

Q

Quartet in F minor, 37
queerness, 149
questions, 153
quotations, 162, 163, 193, 205, 207, 213

R

Recall, Great, 20, 101, 111
  Little, 101, 117
re-creation, musical, 83, 84
redemption, 201
Reger, Max, 206
rehearsals, 5, 11, 44, 56, 57, 58, 72, 87, 169, 173
repartee, 35, 36, 138
retouching, 80, 81
Revelge, 94, 101
revolutionist, incorrigible, 187
religion, 134, 153
religious allegiance, 201
  conversion, 164
  feelings, 89
  inclinations, 132
  perceptions, 134
religiousness, 148
Rembrandt, 139
Resurrection, 111, 187
Rheingold, 11
Rheinlegendchen, 95, 131
Rhine, 137
riddles of the universe, seven, 142

Riga, 29, 31
Opera, 31
Ring, the, 60
Ringstrasse, 52, 53
Rise Ye Up!, 20
Roller, Alfred, 40, 73, 74
romantic, 88, 98, 159, 189
romantic epoch, 202
idiom, 163
scenery, 189
wilderness, 192
romanticism, 90, 91, 121
romanticist (s), 130, 162, 187, 195
rondo, 102
Roquairol, 138
Rückert, 95, 96
rudeness, 50

S

Sabbath, Witches', 115
salt-mines, 191
Salzburg, 191
Salzkammergut, 191, 192
Scheiden und Meiden, 95
scherzi, 99, 109
scherzo literature, 99
Schiele, Egon, 203
Schildwache Nachtlied, Der, 101
Schiller, 145, 160
Schönberg, Arnold, 49, 203, 206, 207, 213
Schindler, Alma Maria, 202
Jacob Emil, 202
Schopenhauer, 129, 136
Schoppe, 138
Schubert, 18, 90, 100, 133, 163
Schumann's influence, 91
Scriabin, 206
secco-recitative, 76
Seidl, 170
Selbstgefühl, 94
Semmering, 209
serum, 62
settings, 73
Shakespeare, 139
Shandy, Tristram, 138
Sibelius, 214, 215, 216
Sieglinde, 71
Siegmund, 71
Silly Affair, A, 138
Sinfonia Domestica, 86
sisters (Mahler's), 22, 191
singers, 37, 38
Sommer marschiert ein, Der, 101, 112, 113
sonata, 102, 107
Songs, 91, 93
humorous, 94
piano, 91
of a Traveling Fellow, 16
soldiers', 93
Symphony in, 58
with orchestra, 93
song-like, 96
song-style, 96
sorrow, world-, 95, 107, 128, 132, 139
soulfulness, 80
Soul Life of the Plants, 139
Spinoza, 123
St. Anthony's Sermon to the Fish, 16
St. Florian Abbey, 162
St. John's Day, 68
Stadtpark, 45
"star" system, 182
Stefan, Paul, 220
Steinbach, 24, 27, 191
Stern Sining Society, 19
Sterne, 138, 139

Strauss, Richard, 86, 193, 195, 196, 206
String Quartet in F minor, 37
style, problems of operatic, 40
  elements of, 73
  late romantic, 159
  musico-dramatic, 181
  problematics of, 114
  Sibelius's, 216
stylistic criteria, 189
Styria, 100
success, 144, 145
Südsturm, 113
"summons," 19, 29
Supreme Being, 164
surrealism, 191, 193
surrealistic devices, 214, 215
Susanna, 72
Swan-chorus, 53
Swabia, Ernest Duke of, 159
Sybilline books, 152
syncretism, dialectical, 197
symphonic, ability, 119
  application, 97
  artist, 98, 124
  composition, 98
  conception, 90
  context, 193
  forms, 89, 97, 124, 137, 164, 190, 213, 215, 216
  gradations, 120
  idea, 89
  ideal, 213
  intentions, 98
  melodies, 96
  movement, 122
  music, 167
  musician, 111
  Poem, 193, 195, 196
symphonic (*Continued*)
  spirit, 164
  style, 168, 216
  tradition, 215
  utterances, 147
  work, 204
  world-dream, 28
Symphonie Phantastique, 115
symphony, classic, 98, 216
  in Songs, 58
  Ninth (Beethoven), 37
  Nordic, 91, 159
  of a Thousand, 56
  Resurrection, 187
  the old, 215
  Third (Bruckner), 164
  Tragic, 48, 120
Symphonies, Mahler's
  First, 3, 16, 89, 95, 98, 100, 105, 106, 108, 110, 118, 123, 137, 173, 187, 195
  Second, 19, 54, 89, 90, 94, 98, 99, 101, 107, 108, 110, 116–8, 122, 131, 187, 190
  Third, 23, 24, 27, 47, 48, 95, 99, 100, 101, 112, 116, 117, 118, 148, 192, 193
  Fourth, 45, 46, 47, 48, 95, 99, 100, 101, 103, 117–9, 146, 204
  Fifth, 45, 47, 99, 101, 102, 104, 119, 120, 125, 150, 205, 206
  Sixth, 45, 48, 98, 99, 101, 102, 120, 125, 150, 206
  Seventh, 45, 56, 98, 99, 101, 102, 120, 121, 125, 150, 206

Symphonies, Mahler's (*Continued*)
Eighth, 45, 56, 102, 121, 122, 150, 212
Ninth, 54, 58, 59, 98, 100, 102, 103, 125, 147, 151, 153, 208, 212, 213
Tenth, 219

T

Tales of Hoffmann, 37, 77
Taming of the Shrew, 39, 76, 77
Tambourgesell, Der, 99, 101
Tannhäuser, 15
Tasso, 130
Tenth Symphony, 219
Titan, 3, 137, 195
"that other world," 120
thematic core, 89
constructions, 97
inexhaustibility, 140
material, 94, 124, 173, 207, 214
statements, 216
thematics, 90, 97, 98, 99
plastic, 102
symphonic, 99
thirties, the catastrophic, 211
Thousand, Symphony of a, 56
Toblach, 56, 57, 61, 208
Tolstoi, 123, 153
"To make naughty children be good," 16
Totes Gebirge, 192
Tragedy, Birth of, 109
Tragic Symphony, 48
Traveling Fellow, Songs of a, 16
Traviata, 12
Trinklied vom Jammer der Erde, 122
Tristan, 12, 35, 40, 73, 74
Tristram Shandy, 138
Tyrol, 57
Southern, 208
twenties, the late, 210, 213

U

Um Mitternacht, 95
unity, 73
United States, 55, 147
Universal Edition, 220
universality, 167, 197, 198
universalism, 199, 216
universe, 192
seven riddles of the, 142
universities, European, 162
University of Vienna, 159, 160, 162
Urlicht, 94

V

variant, 103
variations, 100, 103, 104
Haydn, 103
Veni Creator Spiritus, 102, 121
Verlorene Müh, 95
Vienna, 12, 19, 30, 45–8, 54–7, 59, 63, 68, 69, 80, 85, 100, 158–9, 160, 162, 168, 177, 197, 200–4, 209, 212, 214, 218
Vienna Conservatory, 160
Philharmonic, 19, 20, 37
Vienna's musical supremacy, 198
intellectual climate, 199
Viennese, 35
school, new, 207

Viennese (*Continued*)
"softness," 41
viola-da-gamba, 134

W

Wagner, 11, 35, 69, 71, 76, 77, 81, 84, 126, 142, 159, 162, 164, 180, 181, 189
Wagner addict, 168
disciple, 170
frenzy, 12
Wagnerian drama, 75
leanings, 160
post-, 190
pre-, 189
Wagnerianism, 12
Wagner's baton, 84
death, 168
doctrine, 181
personality, 84
substance, 84
Walküre, 40
waltz, 100, 199
War and Peace, 123
Was mir die Blumen auf der Wiese erzählen, 112
das Felsgebirg erzählt, 24, 113
die Liebe erzählt, 112, 148
die Morgenglocken erzählen, 112
die Nacht erzählt, 112
die Tiere im Walde erzählen, 112
wave, the last, 142
Weber, Carl Maria von, 77, 171
Weber-conscious, 171
Weber's grandson, 171
inventiveness, 172
style, 172
Weimar, 3, 195
Wer hat dies Liedlein erdacht, 95
Werther, 105
White Lady, 39, 77
widow, 209
Wiener Hofoper, 30–34, 36
will-to-do, 147
"will to the other," 85
Witches' Sabbath, 115
Wo die schönen Trompeten blasen, 94
World Beyond, 134
-dream, symphonic, 28
-evil, 132
-sorrow, 95, 107, 128, 132, 139
War, first, 214
Wörthersee, 208
Wotan, 68
Wright, Frank Lloyd, 203

Y

Years of Indiscretion, 138
youthful works, 91
Youth's Magic Horn, 92, 93, 110, 115, 146, 185, 188, 189, 204

Z

"Zahlen!", 15
Zarathustra, 136
Zemlinsky, 49
Zend-Avesta, 135
"Zukunftsmusik," 160
Zu Strassburg auf der Schanz, 93
zwei blauen Augen von meinem Schatz, Die, 95